THE NEW RULERS OF THE WORLD

John Pilger, an Australian, has twice won British journalism's highest award, that of Journalist of the Year, for his work all over the world, especially as a war correspondent. For his documentary film-making, he has won France's Reporter sans Frontières, an American television Academy Award, an 'Emmy', and the Richard Dimbleby Award, given by the British Academy of Film and Television Arts, for a lifetime's factual broadcasting. He lives in London.

THE NEW RULERS
OF THE WORLD

JOHN PILGER

VERSO

London • New York

First published by Verso 2002

1 3 5 7 9 10 8 6 4 2

Verso
UK: 6 Meard Street, London W1F 0EG
USA: 180 Varick Street, New York NY 10014–4606
www.versobooks.com

Verso is the imprint of New Left Books

ISBN 1–85984–393–X

British Library Cataloguing in Publication Data
A catalogue record for this book is
available from the British Library

Library of Congress Cataloging-in-Publication Data
A catalog record for this book is
available from the Library of Congress

Typeset in Perpetua by M Rules
Printed in the UK by The Bath Press, Avon
Printed in Australia by Griffin Press

For Denis Halliday, Hans Von Sponeck, Felicity Arbuthnot, the late Charlie Perkins, Daniel Indra Kusuma, Dita Sari and others too numerous to mention, whose actions have given us power

CONTENTS

ACKNOWLEDGEMENTS

I would like to express my appreciation to these people for their help, directly and indirectly, with this book: Steve Anderson, Anthony Arnove, Joe Bentley, William Blum, Carmel Budiardjo, Scott Burchill, Gabriel Carlysle, Robert Cavanagh, Noam Chomsky, Michel Chossudovsky, Preston Clothier, Barry Coates, Gilly Coote, Mark Curtis, Norm Dixon, Oliver Doward, David Edwards, Susan George, Karl Grossman, Sean Healy, Eric Herring, Pip Hinman, Lynn Hodgkinson, Mike Holderness, Dave Holmes, Laurelle Keough, Max Lane, Alan Lowery, Michael McKinley, Emily Mann, Michael Mansell, Chris Martin, Arthur and Leila Murray, Richard Murray, Lorraine Nelson, David O'Shea, Milan Rai, Grant Roberts, Vicki Robinson, Peter Schumpeter, Bradley Simpson, Colin Tatz, Peter Wilby, Jeffrey Winters. My special thanks go to Jacqueline Korn, Tariq Ali, who gave me the idea, Jane Hindle and Gavin Everall of Verso, Jill Chisholm of the *New Statesman* and Helen Oldfield of *The Guardian*, and Jane Hill, my superb editor and comrade.

INTRODUCTION

When American Vice-President Dick Cheney said that the 'war on terrorism' could last for fifty years or more, his words evoked George Orwell's great prophetic work, *Nineteen Eighty-Four*. We are to live with the threat and illusion of endless war, it seems, in order to justify increased social control and state repression, while great power pursues its goal of global supremacy. Washington is transformed into 'chief city of Airstrip One' and every problem is blamed on the 'enemy', the evil Goldstein, as Orwell called him.[1] He could be Osama bin Laden, or his successors, the 'axis of evil'.

In the novel, three slogans dominate society: war is peace, freedom is slavery and ignorance is strength. Today's slogan, 'war on terrorism', also reverses meaning. The war *is* terrorism. The most potent weapon in this 'war' is pseudo-information, different only in form from that Orwell described, consigning to oblivion unacceptable truths and historical sense. Dissent is permissible within 'consensual' boundaries, reinforcing the illusion that information and speech are 'free'.

The attacks of September 11, 2001 did not 'change everything', but accelerated the continuity of events, providing an extraordinary pretext for destroying social democracy. The undermining of the Bill of Rights in the United States and the further dismantling of trial by jury in Britain and a plethora of related civil liberties are part of the reduction of democracy to electoral ritual: that is, competition between indistinguishable parties for the management of a single-ideology state.

Central to the growth of this 'business state' are the media conglomerates, which have unprecedented power, owning press and television, book publishing, film production and databases. They provide a virtual world of the 'eternal present', as *Time* magazine called it: politics by media, war by media, justice by media, even grief by media (Princess Diana).

The 'global economy' is their most important media enterprise. 'Global economy' is a modern Orwellian term. On the surface, it is instant financial trading, mobile phones, McDonald's, Starbucks, holidays booked on the net. Beneath this gloss, it is the globalisation of poverty, a world where most human beings never make a phone call and live on less than two dollars a day, where 6,000 children die every day from diarrhoea because most have no access to clean water.[2]

In this world, unseen by most of us in the global north, a sophisticated system of plunder has forced more than ninety countries into 'structural adjustment' programmes since the eighties, widening the divide between rich and poor as never before. This is known as 'nation building' and 'good governance' by the 'quad' dominating the World Trade Organisation (the United States, Europe, Canada and Japan) and the Washington triumvirate (the World Bank, the IMF and the US Treasury) that controls even minute aspects of government policy in developing countries. Their power derives largely from an unrepayable debt that forces the poorest countries to pay $100 million to western creditors every day. The result is a world where an elite of fewer than a billion people controls 80 per cent of humanity's wealth.

Promoting this are the transnational media corporations, American and European, that own or manage the world's principal sources of news and information. They have transformed much of the 'information society' into a media age where extraordinary technology allows the incessant repetition of politically 'safe' information that is acceptable to the 'nation builders'. In the West, we are trained to view other societies in terms of their usefulness or threat to 'us' and to regard 'cultural' differences as more important than the political and economic forces by which we judge ourselves. Those with unprecedented resources to understand this, including many who teach and research in the great universities, suppress their knowledge publicly; perhaps never before has there been such a silence.

The New Rulers of the World sets out to explain something of this new 'order' and the importance of breaking the silence that protects great power and its manipulations, notably the current 'war'. There are four essays, beginning with 'The Model Pupil'. This is the story of how the 'global economy' in Asia was spawned in the bloodbath that brought General Suharto to power in Indonesia in 1965–66. It draws on recently released documents that describe a remarkable meeting in 1967 of the world's most powerful corporate figures, at which they carved up the Indonesian economy, sector by sector.

'This was done in the most spectacular way,' Jeffrey Winters, professor at Northwestern University, Chicago, told me. 'They divided up into five different sections: mining in one room, services in another, light industry in another, banking and finance in another . . . You had these big corporate people going around the table, saying [to Suharto's people] this is what we need: this, this and this, and they basically designed the legal infrastructure for investment in Indonesia.'[3]

As a result, a mountain of copper and gold, nickel and bauxite, was handed out to American transnational companies. A group of American, Japanese and French companies got the tropical forests of Sumatra; and so on. I asked one of Suharto's representatives at the 1967 meeting, Emil Salim, if anyone had mentioned that up to a million people had died violently in bringing the new 'global economy' to Indonesia. 'No, that was not on the agenda,' he replied. 'We didn't have television then.'[4]

The greatest massacre of the second half of the twentieth century was not so much news as cause for celebration. The world's fourth most populous country was 'ours'. Suharto's ascendancy was 'the West's best news in years'. James Reston, the doyen of American columnists, told readers of the *New York Times* that the bloody events in Indonesia were 'a gleam of light in Asia'.[5]

In our universities, Indonesian scholars approved Suharto's big lie about a 'communist coup' being the cause of the killings, while western corporations anointed his regime's 'stability'. The silence lasted more than a quarter of a century, until it was broken by the cries of Suharto's victims in East Timor: a second genocide conducted with western military backing.

This chapter draws on my documentary film, *The New Rulers of the World*, broadcast in 2001, from which this book's title is taken. 'New' needs qualifying. The narrative that links all four chapters is the legacy of the 'old' imperialism and its return to respectability as 'globalisation' and the 'war on terrorism'. The 'new rulers' are sometimes misunderstood to be the great transnational corporations, mostly American, that dominate 'world trade'. Certainly, their enormity and scale of operations are new, with the Ford Motor Company now bigger than the economy of South Africa and General Motors wealthier than Denmark.

However, the widely held belief among anti-globalisation campaigners that the state has 'withered away' is misguided, along with the view that transnational corporate power has replaced the state and, by extension, imperialism. As the Russian dissident economist Boris Kagarlitsky points out, 'Globalisation does not mean the impotence of the state, but the rejection by the state of its social functions, in favour of repressive ones, and the ending of democratic freedoms.'[6]

The chapter 'The Great Game' seeks to illuminate the ways in which this disguised state power provides the conditions and privileges that protect western markets while allowing western corporations to intervene where they like in the world, as they did in Indonesia. Today, the imperial state's enduring power is both as 'hidden hand' and iron fist of rampant capital.

The capacity of the American military machine to smash impoverished countries is undisputed, conditional on the absence of American ground troops and their substitution by local or allied forces. The exception was Vietnam. Regardless of their B-52 bombers, napalm, chemical defoliants and weight of numbers, American troops could not match the knowledge and tenacity of a people prepared to see off an invader. This was their imperial lesson.

Thus, in Afghanistan, to date only a handful of Americans have been killed. *Mujaheddin* commanders reported B-52s destroying villages 'too small to be marked on any map', with 'perhaps more than 300 people killed' in one night. In a family of forty, only a small boy and his grandmother survived, reported Richard Lloyd Parry of the *Independent*.[7] Out of sight of the television cameras, 'at least 3,767 civilians were killed by US bombs between October 7 and December 10 . . . an average of sixty-two innocent deaths a day', according to one study; and this in a country whose last annual budget – $83 million – was one-tenth the cost of a B-52 bomber.[8]

This has been reported in the supporting media as a 'vindication', a triumph of ideas, of good over evil, with editorialists and the usual windbag columnists calling for apologies from those who defied the propaganda. At the time of writing, not a single member of the al-Qa'ida leadership, including the Chief Demon bin Laden, has been captured or, to anyone's knowledge, killed. Neither has the Secondary Demon Mullah Omah, leader of the Taliban, been sprung. Indeed, none of those directly implicated in the September 11 attack on America was Afghan; most were Saudis, trained in Germany and the United States, and none has been brought to justice; yet thousands of innocent people in dusty, unseen villages have been subjected to capital punishment without trial, Texas-style, and many more will be maimed over the years by tens of thousands of unexploded cluster bombs.

Moreover, the change in Afghanistan itself is minimal. Women still dare not go unveiled, and warring feudalism reigns. 'The Taliban used to hang the victim's body in public for four days,' said the new, American-installed regime's Minister of Justice. 'We will only hang the body for a short time, say fifteen minutes, after a public execution.'[9]

Describing this as a triumph is like lauding the superiority of the German war machine as a vindication of Nazism.

In the media age, ignorance is strength and omission standard practice. Mere examination of the root causes of September 11 invites smear. David McKnight, an Australian journalist and academic, wrote that 'people like John Pilger and Noam Chomsky appear to absolve the [September 11] perpetrators of their crime'.[10] I had written in *The*

Guardian: 'The truth [about September 11] is that the killing of thousands of innocent people is not justified in America, or anywhere else.'[11] To McKnight and those he echoes, the killing of thousands of innocents in Afghanistan is 'the global equivalent of police raiding the hide-out of the criminal', involving 'a violent confrontation that is sometimes unavoidable in apprehending criminals'.

That Afghan peasants have the same right to life as New Yorkers is unmentionable, a profanity. The murderous demolition of their villages, with not a Taliban or al-Qa'ida fighter in sight, is 'unavoidable'. In other words, certain human lives have greater worth than others and the killing of only one set of civilians is a crime. The terrorists of Osama bin Laden and George W Bush are sustained by this ancient lie.

They are also joined by history. The CIA's 'Operation Cyclone' trained and armed at least 35,000 zealots who became the Taliban and al-Qa'ida.[12] As John Cooley writes in his definitive *Unholy Wars: Afghanistan, America and International Terrorism*, 'Prime Minister Margaret Thatcher's Government supported the [American-funded] *jihad* with full enthusiasm', much of it co-ordinated by an MI6 officer in Islamabad. Osama bin Laden was given 'full rein'.[13] The cost to the American tax-payer was $4 billion. Rescuing these facts ought to be the job of journalists and scholars, but this has not happened.

At the height of the bombing of Afghanistan, the *Observer* paid tribute to its great publisher and editor, David Astor, who had died. In opposing the British attack on Suez in 1956, Astor, said the paper, 'took the Government to task for its bullying and in so doing defined the *Observer* as a freethinking paper prepared to swim against the tide of popular sentiment.' Astor had described 'an endeavour to reimpose nineteenth-century imperialism of the

crudest kind'. He wrote: 'Nations are said to have the governments they deserve. Let us show that we deserve better.' The
Observer commented that 'the richness of the language and rele-
vance of the sentiments resonate today'.[14] The words were almost
surreal, the irony exquisite. The *Observer* supported the Blair
Government's 'endeavour' in Afghanistan.

This book continues a strand in my earlier books, *Heroes*, *Distant
Voices* and *Hidden Agendas*, which compared the actions of politicians
in western democracies with those of criminal tyrants. In cause and
effect, the crucial difference is distance from the carnage, and the
dissemination of an insidious propaganda that says a crime is not a
crime if 'we' commit it. It was not a crime to murder more than
half a million peasants with bombs dropped secretly and illegally on
Cambodia, igniting an Asian holocaust. It was not a crime for Bill
Clinton and George W Bush, Tony Blair and his Tory predecessors
to have caused the deaths in Iraq of 'more people than have been
killed by all weapons of mass destruction in history', to quote the
conclusion of an American study.[15]

Their medieval blockade against twenty-two million people,
now in its twelfth year, is the subject of the chapter 'Paying the
Price'. The facts are not in dispute, though rarely published. A
report by the United Nations Secretary-General in October 2001
says that the obstruction of $4 billion of humanitarian supplies by
the US and British governments is by far the main cause of the
extreme suffering and deaths in Iraq. The United Nations
Children's Fund, Unicef, says that every month up to 6,000 children die mostly as a result of the blockade.[16] This is twice the total
number of deaths in the Twin Towers and another vivid reminder
of the different value of different lives. The Twin Towers victims
are people. The Iraqi children are unpeople.

At the time of writing, Iraq is likely to be attacked by the US. Using sections of the American and British press as 'conduits', American intelligence has successfully created what the CIA in Indochina used to call a 'master illusion'. This is the threat of Iraq's 'weapons of mass destruction'. There is no proof or credible evidence of any such threat, which has been denied by the former United Nations inspector in Iraq, Scott Ritter.[17]

However, the Iraqi 'threat' is central to the Bush administration's post-September 11 strategy of 'total war'. Defence Secretary Donald Rumsfeld's instructions to the Pentagon to 'think the unthinkable' may well cause non-Americans, at least, to worry that the world's only superpower has been taken over by fundamentalists whose fanaticism promises human carnage on a scale that makes amateurs of the Taliban.[18]

In Washington, the 'oil group' under George W Bush and Vice-President Cheney (George Bush Senior, like Cheney and others in his Cabinet, was a consultant to the Carlyle Group, which advised the bin Laden family) is increasingly influenced by the Defense Policy Board (DPB), a semi-official panel that advises Rumsfeld and his deputy, Paul Wolfowitz. Known in Washington as the 'Wolfowitz cabal', the group draws together the extreme right of American political life and is responsible for the inspiration behind the 'war on terrorism', principally a concept of 'total war'.

One of the group's 'thinkers', Richard Perle, a cold war planner in the Reagan administration, offered this explanation. 'No stages,' he said. 'This is total war. We are fighting a variety of enemies. There are lots of them out there. All this talk about first we are going to do Afghanistan, then we will do Iraq, then we take a look around and see how things stand. This is entirely the wrong way to go about it . . . If we just let our vision of the world go forth, and we embrace it entirely, and we don't try to piece together clever diplomacy, but just wage a total war . . . our children will sing great songs about us years from now.'[19]

The pursuit of the criminals of September 11 is not enough. 'Terrorism' demands endless war. A replacement for the 'red scare' has at last been found, justifying a permanent war footing and paranoia, and construction of the greatest military machine ever: the 'National Defense Missile Programme'. This, says the US Space Command, will ensure the 'full spectrum dominance' of the world.[20]

This means complete military mastery, which is likened in Pentagon literature to the European navies' dominance of both the northern and eastern hemispheres in the nineteenth century. It does not end there. These words are already applied in other areas, notably the control of all economic life, the composition, or 'internal wiring', as the *New York Times* put it, of foreign governments and the redefinition of dissent as an 'international security concern'.

This is expressed more openly and crudely than ever before, notably by a select group of literate oafs in the American press. In an article entitled 'Unilateralism is the key to our success', Charles Krauthammer of the *Washington Post* described the world in the next fifty years as one without protection against nuclear attack or environmental damage for the citizens of any country except the United States; a world where 'democracy' means nothing if its benefits are at odds with American 'interests'; a world in which to express dissent against these 'interests' brands one a terrorist and justifies surveillance, repression and death.[21] As Drew Whitworth pointed out, these beliefs are indistinguishable from those of Osama bin Laden, 'carried forward by a few men without a mandate'.[22]

There is an echo of the 'Thousand Year Reich' about this, first promoted in an American context by Henry Luce's bellicose proclamation, in 1941 in *Time*, of an 'American Century'. In the United States, academic-populists once again dispense a *Reader's Digest* view of the world, such as Samuel Huntington's *Clash of Civilisations* and, more recently, Victor Davis Hanson's *Why the West Has Won*, with its call to 'civic militarism'.[23] In none of these texts, which emphasise 'cultural' supremacy, is there recognition that the imperialist imperatives of the American Century have undermined the greatest western achievement, that of secular, redistributive politics, and allowed the maelstrom stemming from American violence, along with introspective, revengeful religion, to fill the gaps.

This book argues that we urgently need antidotes to a propaganda that beckons dangers no less than those of the cold war.

We need an awareness of lethal double standards: that 'international law' and 'international community' are often merely the preserves of great power, not the expression of the majority. The United States can mount a posse (known as a 'coalition') to attack countries, while the numerous UN General Assembly resolutions calling for justice in Palestine are not worth the paper they are written on. We also need to examine the common use of 'we' and its appropriation by great power. If 'we' are to fight terrorism, then 'we' must call on the United States to end its terror in the Middle East, Colombia and elsewhere. Only then can 'we' make the world a safer place.

The final chapter, 'The Chosen Ones', which contrasts Olympian imagery with the reality of indigenous lives in my own country, Australia, follows on from and borrows from my 1989 book, *A Secret Country*, and my 1999 film, *Welcome to Australia*. I have been writing about and filming the struggle of the Aboriginal people for more than thirty years; and I am still moved and shocked by the unresolved apartheid behind the picture postcard of Australia.

A universal breaking of silence is exemplified in the Aboriginal struggle. The reawakening among many Aborigines, in politics, the law and the arts especially, is the achievement of some of the most tenacious and courageous activists anywhere. They are Renaissance men and women, who face one of the most intransigent and meanest political establishments. Sometimes, emerging from yet another meeting with nodding politicians, they lose heart; and, like so many of their young people, die by their own hand. Rob Riley, a courageous indigenous leader, was one who died this way.

One of my oldest friends, Charlie Perkins, Australia's Martin Luther King, lived past the age of sixty, an amazing achievement for one whose people more often than not die in their thirties and forties. It was Charlie who led the 'freedom rides' of the sixties into Australia's equivalent of the American Deep South, chaining himself to the turnstiles of swimming pools that refused to admit black children. His last, long interview with me is published here.

On our first visit to Alice Springs together, in 1969, Charlie's mother, Hetti, who was a queen of the Arrente people, suggested we gain entry to an Aboriginal 'reserve', a concentration camp in the bush, by revving the car and ramming the gate, which we did. This book is a tribute to those, like Charlie and Hetti, whose actions shame the silent and defy the myth of apathy.

They represent worldwide movements of people with little: in India the 300,000-strong, all-female Self Employed Women's Association (SEWA); in Brazil the Landless People's Movement; in Mexico the Zapatistas. Their victories, usually unrecognised in the West, are often epic. In Bolivia's third city, Cochabamba, ordinary people took back their water from a corporate conglomerate, after the World Bank had pressurised the Bolivian government into privatising the public water supply. Having refused credit to the public water company, the bank demanded that a monopoly be given to Aguas del Tunari, part of International Water Limited, a British-based company half-owned by the American engineering giant Bechtel.

Granted a forty-year concession, the company immediately raised the price of water. In a country where the minimum wage is less than $100 a month, people faced increases in their water bills of $20 a month – more than water users pay each month in the wealthy suburbs of Washington, home to many World Bank economists. In Cochabamba, even collecting rainwater without a permit was now illegal.

So they organised; young and old, activists and those who, as Marcela Lopez Levy wrote, had previously been 'too busy surviving to get involved'. She spoke to Marcelo Rojas, who became one of the leaders. 'I had never taken an interest in politics before,' he said. 'My father is a politician, and I thought it was all about cutting deals. But to see people fighting for their water, their rights, made me realise there was a common good to defend, that the country can't be left in the hands of the politicians.' He was arrested and tortured by the police, as were many young people who built barricades and protected the old when the authorities attacked. They took over their city and they won. The government tore up the contract, and the company cleared its desks.[24]

Epic victories of that kind, all over the world, are not part of the media agenda. Argentina is reported as chaos, not as a struggle with connections to our own lives. The struggle of journalists in Turkey for a free press, of trade unionists in Colombia and the new 'tiger' unions in East Asia are little known in the West. In Indonesia, the IMF may have delivered an expedient *coup de grâce* to the genocidist Suharto, but it was extraordinarily brave people, like Dita Sari and

Daniel Indra Kusuma, to whom this book is dedicated, who broke the long silence and faced guns and armoured vehicles supplied by the dictator's friends, notably the British government.

In South Africa, it was young people, like those at Soweto in 1976, who faced the 'Hippos', the hideous armoured vehicles from which the police killed and wounded indiscriminately. Study Paul Weinberg's historic photograph of a lone woman standing defiant between two of these monsters, as they rolled into her township; her arms are raised, her fists are clenched. The negotiators played a part, but it was those like her who defeated apartheid.[25]

The list is endless and a source of optimism in these politically surreal times. Contrary to myth, people are seldom compliant. In a survey of thirty countries, Gallup found that the majority opposed the bombing of Afghanistan and military violence as a means of bringing terrorists to justice.[26] For all the propaganda of 'news', the attempts to turn state murder into a morality play, people remain sceptical, at least. There is a critical public intelligence, which journalists would do well to respect. That the real terror is poverty, from which some 24,000 people die every day, is beyond public dispute.[27]

Following September 11, Robin Theurkauf, a lecturer in international law at Yale University, wrote, 'Terrorist impulses ferment in poverty, oppression and ignorance. The elimination of these conditions and the active promotion of a universal respect for human rights must become a priority.'

She lost her husband, Tom, in the Twin Towers.[28]

John Pilger, February 2002

THE MODEL PUPIL

With its 100 million people and its 300-mile arc of islands containing the region's richest hoard of natural resources, Indonesia is the greatest prize in South-East Asia.

Richard Nixon, 1967

Flying into Jakarta, it is not difficult to imagine the city below fitting the World Bank's description of Indonesia. A 'model pupil of globalisation' was the last of many laurels the bank bestowed. That was almost four years ago. Within weeks, short-term global capital had fled the country, the stock market and currency had crashed, and the number of people living in absolute poverty had reached almost 70 million. The next year, 1998, General Suharto was forced to resign after thirty years as dictator, taking with him severance pay estimated at $15 billion, the equivalent of almost 13 per cent of his country's foreign debt, much of it owed to the World Bank.[1]

From the air, it is the industrial design of the city that is striking. Jakarta is ringed by vast, guarded, relatively modern compounds, known as export processing zones, or EPZs. These enclose hundreds of factories that make products for foreign companies: the clothes people buy on the high street in Britain, in shopping malls in north America and Australia: from the high-street designer look of Gap to the Nike, Adidas and Reebok trainers that sell in London's Oxford Street for up to £100 a pair. In these factories are thousands of workers earning the equivalent of seventy-two pence a day, about a dollar. This is the official minimum wage in Indonesia, which, says the government, is about half the living wage; and here, that means subsistence, bordering on a working pauperism. Nike workers get about 4 per cent of the retail price of the shoes they make, which is not enough to buy the laces. Still, they count themselves lucky: they have jobs. The 'booming, dynamic economic success' (another World Bank accolade) has left more than 36 million Indonesians without work.

Posing as a London fashion buyer (for the filming of my ITV documentary *The New Rulers of the World*[2]) I was given a tour of one such factory, which makes Gap clothes for Britain and America. I found more than a thousand mostly young women working, battery-style, under the glare of strip lighting, in temperatures that reach 40 degrees Centigrade. The only air-conditioning was upstairs, where the Taiwanese bosses were. What struck me was the claustrophobia, the sheer frenzy of the production and a fatigue and sadness that were like a presence. The faces were silent, the eyes downcast; limbs moved robotically. The women have no choice about the hours they must work, including a notorious 'long shift': 36 hours without going home. I was assured that, if I wanted to place a last-minute order, that was 'no problem' because 'we just make the workers stay longer'.

The workers I met later, secretly, told me: 'If Gap trousers have to be finished, we don't leave. We stay till the order is full, no matter the time. If you want to go to the toilet, you have to be lucky. If the supervisor says no, you shit in your pants . . . we are treated like animals because we have to work hard all the time without saying a word.'

I told them the Gap company boasted about a 'code of conduct' that protected workers' basic rights.

'We've never seen it,' they said. 'Foreigners from Gap come to the factory, but they are interested only in quality control and the rate of production. They never ask about working conditions. They don't even look at us.'

Clinging to the factories, like the debris of a great storm, are the labour camps where these workers live: Hobbesian communities crammed in long dormitories made from breeze blocks, plywood packing cases and corrugated iron. Like the majority of humanity who are not touched by the delights of McDonald's and Starbucks, the internet and mobile phones, who cannot afford to eat enough protein and rarely make a phone call, these are globalisation's unpeople. They live with open, overflowing sewers and unsafe water; up to half their wage goes on drinkable water. Past their homes run stinking canals dug by the former colonial masters, the Dutch, in the usual vainglorious attempt to re-create Europe in Asia.

The result is an urban environmental disaster that breeds mosquitoes; today, a plague of them in the camps has brought a virulent form of dengue fever, known as 'break-back fever'. After several visits here, I was bitten and took two months to recover from the infection. For the undernourished young children in the camps, dengue can mean death. It is a disease of globalisation; as the camps grew and people migrated from rural areas looking for work, the mosquitoes followed them. Many of the people had fled an impoverishing system of cash-cropping, devised by the World Bank, and which has progressively wiped out self-sustaining agriculture in much of Indonesia.

I could just squeeze along one of the passageways. Filled with clothes hanging in plastic, it was like the backroom of a dry cleaner's. The cleanliness and neatness of the people living in this warren is astonishing. They occupy cell-like rooms, mostly without windows or ventilation, in which eating and sleeping are tuned to the ruthless rhythm of shiftwork in the factories. During the monsoon season, the canals rise and flood, and more plastic materialises to protect possessions: a precious tape player, posters of the Spice Girls and Che Guevara. I almost tipped over a frying pan of sizzling tofu. There are open paraffin fires and children darting perilously close. I watched a family of five perched on a patch of green, gazing at the sunset through a polluted yellow haze; tiny bats circled overhead and in the distance were the skeletal silhouettes of deserted skyscrapers. It was an apocalyptic glimpse of a 'globalised' world unknown to those of us who 'consume'.

The 'code of conduct', which the San Francisco-based Gap company says it distributes to its contractors, includes this: 'Dormitory facilities [must] meet all applicable laws and regulations related to health and safety, including fire safety, sanitation, risk protection and electrical, mechanical and structural safety.'[3] Because these dormitories are not on the factory site, Gap and its contractors are not liable. Consumers in the West might reflect on this non-liability as they pay for fashionable clothes made by people who cannot afford a decent place to live on the wages they are paid.

Ten miles from the camps, along a toll road owned by Suharto's daughter (he distributed the national power grid among his children; banks, hotels and vast tracts of forest were tossed to generals and other cronies), lies downtown Jakarta. This is, or was, the approved face of the global 'model pupil'. There are shopping malls with Versace leather coats priced at £2,000, and a showroom of Jaguar cars, and a vast McDonald's with sugar-plump children perched on Ronald's plastic knee. One of the smartest hotels is the Shangri-La. Four wedding receptions are held here every Sunday night. I attended one that cost $120,000. It was held in the grand ballroom, which is a local version of the ballroom of the Waldorf Astoria in New York, complete with chandeliers and gold-leaf arches. The guests wore Armani, Versace and real diamonds, and dropped cheques in a large box. The couple were from rich Chinese families, although their names were Joe and Francesca. (When he seized power, Suharto banned Chinese names and Chinese writing; he apparently associated Chinese with communism.) There was an eight-tier cake and the initials of the couple carved in ice; and holiday snaps of their world tour were projected cinema-size. The guests included former cronies of the deposed dictator, such as an infamous crook who made his fortune in occupied East Timor; also present was the chief representative of the World Bank in Indonesia, Mark Baird, a New Zealander, who looked troubled when I asked him if he was enjoying himself. The World Bank emphasises these days that its mission in Indonesia is 'poverty reduction' and 'reaching out to the poor'. It was the World Bank that set up the $86 million loan that built the Shangri-La, which 'would provide the security of regular employment'. Shortly after the wedding attended by Baird, most of the workers were sacked when they went on strike for a living wage.

The Gotham City skyline of downtown Jakarta is mostly banks, many of them empty, and unfinished buildings. Before 1997, there were more banks here than in any city on earth; half of them went bust when the 'dynamic' economy collapsed beneath the weight of its barely credible corruption. During Suharto's thirty-year dicta-torship, a cataract of 'global' capital poured into Indonesia. The World Bank handed out more than $30 billion, some of which went on worthwhile programmes, like literacy. More than $630 million went into a notorious 'transmigration' programme that allowed the regime to colonise the archipelago. Migrants from all over Indonesia were sent to occupied East Timor, where they soon controlled the economy. In 2001, the blood-letting in Kalimantan (Borneo) was directed against Madura islanders who had been shipped in to 'develop' the territory under a World Bank scheme. In August 1997, a secret internal World Bank report, written in Jakarta, disclosed the greatest scandal in the history of 'develop-ment' – that 'at least 20 to 30 per cent' of the bank's loans 'are diverted through informal payments to GOI [Government of Indonesia] staff and politicians'.[4]

During his dictatorship, seldom a day would pass when General Suharto was not being congratulated by western politicians for bringing 'stability' to the world's fifth most populous nation. British politicians were especially appreciative, beginning with Harold Wilson's Foreign Secretary, Michael Stewart, who in 1966 lauded the dictator's 'sensible economic policies' and said his regime was 'not aggressive'.[5] Margaret Thatcher called Suharto 'one of our very best and most valuable friends'. John Major's Foreign Secretary, Douglas Hurd, championed his regime's 'Asian values' (the unctuous code for lack of democracy and abuses of human rights). In 1997, Robin Cook's first trip abroad as Foreign

Secretary included Indonesia, where he shook hands warmly with Suharto: so warmly that a colour photograph of the pair of them was chosen, bizarrely, to illustrate the Foreign Office's report on human rights in the world. Only the Australians, with their complex fears of their Asian neighbours, perceived as about to fall down on them as if by the force of gravity, were more obsequious. Prime Minister Bob Hawke told Suharto, 'We know your people love you.'[6] His successor, Paul Keating, who, the Australian press claimed, looked upon Suharto as a 'father figure', lauded the tyrant for creating a 'tolerant society' and bringing 'stability' to the region.[7] In 1996, the Deputy Prime Minister, Tim Fischer, declared that 'when magazines look for the man of the world of the second half of this century, they perhaps should not look much further than Jakarta.'[8]

They all knew, of course. Amnesty almost filled a room with evidence of Suharto's grisly record. Robin Cook was aware of an exhaustive investigation by the foreign affairs committee of the Australian Parliament that concluded that Suharto's troops had caused the deaths of 'at least' 200,000 East Timorese, a third of the population.[9] In New Labour's first year in office, Britain was the biggest weapons supplier to Indonesia, with Blair approving eleven arms deals with Indonesia under cover of the Official Secrets Act and Cook's declaration of an 'ethical' dimension to foreign policy.[10]

This had a certain logic; the arms trade is one of globalisation's successes, and Indonesia, the 'model pupil', has played a vital role. When the 'global economy' (i.e. unfettered capitalism) took hold in Britain in the early 1980s, Margaret Thatcher set about dismantling much of manufacturing and industry while restoring the British arms industry to a supremacy second only to the United States. This was done with veiled subsidies of the kind that routinely underwrite and rig the 'free market'. Almost half of all research and development funds went on 'defence'; and the Export Credit Guarantee Department of the Department of Trade and Industry offered 'soft loans' to third-world regimes shopping for hi-tech sabres to rattle. That many had appalling human rights records and internal conflict and/or were on the verge of war with a neighbour (India, Pakistan, Iran, Iraq, Israel) was not a barrier. Indonesia was a major recipient of these virtual giveaways. During one twelve-month period, almost £1 billion of ECGD money financed the sale of Hawk fighter-bombers to Indonesia. The unknowing British tax-payer paid up; the arms industry reaped its profits; and the Hawks were used to bomb villages in the mountains of East Timor.[11]

I drove into the Krawang region of Java, where I met a rice farmer called Sarkom. It is fair to describe Sarkom as representative of the 80 per cent of humanity whose livelihoods depend on agriculture. He is not among the poorest; he lives with his wife and three daughters in a small, bamboo-walled house and there are tiles on the floor. At the front, under the eaves, is a bamboo bed, a chair and a table where his wife, Cucuk, supplements their income with sewing.

Last year, the International Monetary Fund offered the post-Suharto government a 'rescue package' of multi-million-dollar loans. The conditions included the elimination of import tariffs on staple foods. 'Trade in all qualities of rice has been opened to general importers and exporters', decreed the IMF's Letter of Intent. Fertilisers and pesticides also lost their 70 per cent subsidy.[12]

This means that farmers like Sarkom are likely to go bankrupt, and their children forced to find work in the cities. Moreover, it gives the green light to the giant American foodgrains corporations to move into Indonesia. The double standard embodied in these conditions is breathtaking. Agribusiness in the West, especially the United States and Europe, has produced its famous surpluses and export power only because of high tariff walls and massive domestic subsidies. The result has been a monopoly on humanity's staples. The chief executive of the Cargill Corporation, which dominates the world trade in foodgrains, boasted, 'When we get up from the breakfast table each morning, much of what we have eaten – cereals, bread, coffee, sugar and so on – has passed through the hands of my company.'[13] Cargill's goal is to double in size every five to seven years.

This is known as 'free trade'.

'I went to prison for fourteen years so that this would not happen,' said Sarkom. 'All my friends, those who were not killed, went to prison so that the power of big money would not take us over. I don't care what they call it now – global this or that. It's the same force, the same threat to our lives.'

His remark opens a chapter in Indonesia's recent past that western politicians and businessmen would prefer to forget, although they have been among its chief beneficiaries. Sarkom was one of tens of thousands imprisoned when General Suharto, an opportunist, seized power in Indonesia in 1965–66, the 'year of living dangerously', eventually deposing the nationalist president Achmed Sukarno, who had led Indonesia since the end of Dutch colonial rule. Estimates of the people who died in a pogrom directed primarily at Indonesia's communist party, the PKI, range from 500,000 to more than a million.

Sarkom was nineteen when he was taken away. He is trying to write down in an exercise book his memories of the horrors he experienced. He was for many years on Buru island, where thousands were imprisoned, at first without housing, food and water. On the day I came to see him, he had gathered a group of friends for me to meet, men in their sixties and seventies, who were also *tapols*, political prisoners released since the fall of Suharto. Two were teachers, one a civil servant, another a member of parliament. One man was imprisoned because he refused to vote for Suharto's front party, Golkar. Several were PKI members. Adon Sutrisna, a teacher, told me, 'We are the people, the nation, that the world forgot. If you know the truth about what happened in Indonesia, you can understand clearly where the world is being led today.'

A few miles from Sarkom's farm is a hump of earth overgrown with mustard flowers, and no markings. It is a mass grave. Thirty-five years after the murders, the families of the victims, believed to be a dozen, are still too frightened to place a headstone. However, in the post-Suharto era, many Indonesians are now overcoming a fear that has consumed a generation; and throughout the countryside families have begun to excavate the remains of their loved ones. They are often furtive figures of the night, occasionally glimpsed on the rim of a paddy, or a riverbank. The older witnesses recall rivers 'jammed with bodies like logs'; in village after village, young men were slaughtered for no reason, their murders marked by rows of severed penises.

I have a friend in Jakarta whose name is Roy. Others call him Daniel. These are two of many aliases that have helped keep him alive since 1965. He belongs to a remarkable group of revolutionaries who went underground during the long years of Suharto's repression, the years when the World Bank was tutoring its 'model pupil', emerging at critical moments to lead spears of a clandestine opposition movement. He was arrested and tortured on several occasions. 'I survived because they never knew it was me,' he said. 'Once a torturer yelled at me, "Tell us where Daniel is!"' In 1998, he helped bring on to the streets the students whose courageous confrontations with the military (using British riot vehicles) played a critical role in bringing down the dictator.

Roy took me back to his primary school, where, for him, the nightmare of Suharto's rule began. We sat in an empty classroom and he recalled the day in October 1965 when he watched a gang burst in and drag the headmaster into the playground, and beat him to death. 'He was a wonderful man: gentle and kind,' he said. 'He would sing to the class, and read to me. He was the person that I, as a boy, looked up to . . . I can hear his screams now, but for a long time, years in fact, all I could remember was running from the classroom, and running and running through the streets, not stopping. When they found me that evening, I was dumbstruck. For a whole year I couldn't speak.'

The headmaster was suspected of being a communist. His murder was typical of systematic executions of teachers, students, civil servants, peasant farmers. 'In terms of the numbers killed,' reported the Central Intelligence Agency, 'the massacres rank as one of the worst mass murders of the 20th century'.[14] The historian Gabriel Kolko wrote that 'the "final solution" to the communist problem in Indonesia ranks as a crime of the same type as the Nazis perpetrated.'[15] According to the Asia specialist Peter Dale Scott, western politicians, diplomats, journalists and scholars, 'some with rather prominent CIA connections', are 'perhaps principally responsible' for the myth that Suharto and the military had

saved the nation's honour from an attempted coup by the
Indonesian communist party, the PKI, whose 'carnage' had caused
a 'spontaneous, popular revulsion'.[16]

Sukarno had relied on the communists as a counterweight to
the army, which, having been trained by the Japanese during the
Second World War, basked in its own mythology as guardian of
the nation. When six army generals were murdered on
September 30, 1965, Suharto blamed the PKI, and it was this
version that dominated his regime's propaganda and the largely
fictional account promoted in the West, not least by the popular novel *The Year of Living Dangerously* by Christopher Koch,
which represented the PKI as an enemy within that 'would
stamp out the ancient dreams which are the spiritual life-blood
of the country'.[17]

The commentary of a prominent Australian academic, Heinz
Arndt, was not exceptional. 'The Suharto Government,' he
wrote, 'is genuinely and desperately anxious not to be thought
undemocratic, militaristic, dictatorial. It wants to educate
and persuade, not to ride roughshod over anyone . . . It is no
mean thing that Indonesia now has a very much more moderate,
more rational, more pragmatic leadership than for many
years . . .'[18] As Scott Burchill points out, 'Considering the
number of historians who have addressed the question, the
extent to which this orthodoxy still prevails is remarkable.'
Burchill quotes Greg Sheridan, foreign editor of *The Australian*
who, as recently as 1998, absolved Suharto as a 'monster of the
Left's imagination'.[19]

Rupert Murdoch's *Australian*, the country's only national newspaper, was an important promoter of the dictator. Sheridan
frequently attacked those who pointed out Suharto's complicity in

human rights abuses. His targets included the foreign affairs committee of the Australian Parliament, for its finding that 'at least 200,000' people had died in East Timor under Suharto's military occupation. He mocked the eyewitnesses to massacres. 'The truth,' he wrote, 'is that even genuine victims frequently concoct stories . . .'[20] At the height of the repression in East Timor, *The Australian*'s Jakarta correspondent, Patrick Walters, wrote that 'no one was now arrested without proper legal procedures'. After all, he had been assured by the puppet governor that 'the situation regarding human rights is very good at the moment'.[21] The editor-in-chief, Paul Kelly, sat on the board of the Australia-Indonesia Institute, a body funded by the Australian government to promote 'common interests' between the two countries. In 1994, Kelly was in Jakarta at Suharto's side, introducing the mass murderer to a respectful line of Australian editors.[22] 'There is no alternative to Suharto,' declared Kelly shortly before the tyrant was finally overthrown, ending a reign his paper had described as 'moderate'.[23]

Since Suharto's fall, a body of evidence has been amassed that exposes the fiction both of the 'moderate' regime and the 'communist carnage' of 1965–66. Witnesses have spoken for the first time and documents have come to light strongly suggesting that Suharto, who had military command of Jakarta, exploited an internecine struggle in order to seize power. Certainly, if it was a 'communist coup', it had a unique feature: none of the officers accused of plotting it was a communist. There is now little doubt that the pogrom that followed was fanned by Suharto and his co-conspirators, and that PKI members and anybody who got in the way were the victims.

What is also no longer in doubt is the collaboration of western governments, together with the subsequent role of western big business. Indeed, it might be said that globalisation in Asia was conceived in Indonesia's bloodbath.

For the British, the immediate goal was to protect their post-colonial interests in Malaysia, then threatened by 'confrontation' with an 'unstable' Sukarno. Sukarno had complained that the formation in 1963 of the Malaysian Federation (Malaya and Singapore) was a 'neo-colonial plot' to further British commercial interests. Foreign Office files, since declassified, reveal that he had a point. A file in 1964 called for the 'defence' of western interests in South-East Asia, 'a major producer of essential commodities. The region produces nearly 85 per cent of the world's natural rubber, over 45 per cent of the tin, 65 per cent of the copra and 23 per cent of the chromium ore.'[24] Moreover, two years earlier, according to a CIA memorandum, Prime Minister Harold Macmillan and President John Kennedy had agreed to 'liquidate President Sukarno, depending on the situation and available opportunities'. The CIA author added, 'It is not clear to me whether murder or overthrow is intended by the word liquidate.'[25]

Sukarno was a populist, the founder of modern Indonesia and of the non-aligned movement of developing countries, which he hoped would forge a genuine 'third way' between the spheres of the two superpowers. In 1955, he convened the 'Asia-Africa Conference' in the Javanese hill city of Bandung. It was the first time the leaders of the developing world, the majority of humanity, had met to forge common interests: a prospect that alarmed the western powers, especially as the vision and idealism of non-alignment represented a potentially popular force that might seriously challenge neo-colonialism. The hopes invested in such an unprecedented meeting are glimpsed in the faded tableaux and black-and-white photographs in the museum at Bandung and in the forecourt of the splendid art deco Savoy Hotel, where the following Bandung Principles are displayed:

1   Respect for fundamental human rights and the principles of the United Nations Charter.
2   Respect for the sovereignty and territorial integrity of all nations.
3   The recognition of the equality of all peoples.
4   The settlement of disputes by peaceful means.

Sukarno could be a democrat and a demagogue. For a time, Indonesia was a parliamentary democracy, then became what he called a 'guided democracy'. He encouraged mass trade unions and peasant, women's and cultural movements. Between 1959 and 1965, more than 15 million people joined political parties or affiliated mass organisations that were encouraged to challenge British and American influence in the region. With 3 million members, the PKI was the largest communist party in the world outside the Soviet Union and China. According to the Australian historian Harold Crouch, 'the PKI had won widespread support not as a revolutionary party but as an organisation defending the interests of the poor within the existing system'.[26] It was this popularity, rather than any armed insurgency, that alarmed the Americans. Like Vietnam to the north, Indonesia might 'go communist'.

In 1990, the American investigative journalist Kathy Kadane revealed the extent of secret American collaboration in the massacres of 1965–66 which allowed Suharto to seize the presidency. Following a series of interviews with former US officials, she wrote, 'They systematically compiled comprehensive lists of communist operatives. As many as 5,000 names were furnished to the Indonesian army, and the Americans later checked off the names of those who had been killed or captured.'[27] One of those interviewed was Robert J Martens, a political officer in the US embassy in Jakarta. 'It was a big help to the army,' he said. 'They probably killed a lot of people and I probably have a lot of blood on my hands, but that's not all bad. There's a time when you have to strike hard at a decisive moment.'[28] Joseph Lazarsky, the deputy CIA station chief in Jakarta, said that confirmation of the killings came straight from Suharto's headquarters. 'We were getting a good account in Jakarta of who was being picked up,' he said. 'The army had a "shooting list" of about 4,000 or 5,000 people. They didn't have enough goon squads to zap them all, and some individuals were valuable for interrogation. The infrastructure [of the PKI] was zapped almost immediately. We knew what they were doing . . . Suharto and his advisers said, if you keep them alive, you have to feed them.'[29]

Having already armed and equipped much of the army, Washington secretly supplied Suharto's troops with a field communications network as the killings got under way. Flown in at night by US air force planes based in the Philippines, this was state-of-the-art equipment, whose high frequencies were known to the CIA and the National Security Agency advising President Johnson. Not only did this allow Suharto's generals to co-ordinate the killings, it meant that the highest echelons of the US administration were listening in and that Suharto could seal off large areas of the country. Although there is archive film of people being herded into trucks and driven away, a single fuzzy photograph of a massacre is, to my knowledge, the only pictorial record of what was Asia's holocaust.[30]

The American Ambassador in Jakarta was Marshall Green, known in the State Department as 'the coupmaster'. Green had arrived in Jakarta only months earlier, bringing with him a reputation for having masterminded the overthrow of the Korean leader Syngman Rhee, who had fallen out with the Americans. When the killings got under way in Indonesia, manuals on student organising, written in Korean and English, were distributed by the US embassy to the Indonesian Student Action Command (KAMI), whose leaders were sponsored by the CIA.

On October 5, 1965, Green cabled Washington on how the United States could 'shape developments to our advantage'. The plan was to blacken the name of the PKI and its 'protector', Sukarno. The propaganda should be based on '[spreading] the story of the PKI's guilt, treachery and brutality'. At the height of the bloodbath, Green assured General Suharto: 'The US is generally sympathetic with and admiring of what the army is doing.'[31] As for the numbers killed, Howard Federspiel, the Indonesia expert at the State Department's Bureau of Intelligence and Research in 1965, said, 'No one cared, as long as they were communists, that they were being butchered. No one was getting very worked up about it.'[32]

The Americans worked closely with the British, the reputed masters and inventors of the 'black' propaganda admired and adapted by Joseph Goebbels in the 1930s. Sir Andrew Gilchrist, the Ambassador in Jakarta, made his position clear in a cable to the Foreign Office: 'I have never concealed from you my belief that a little shooting in Indonesia would be an essential preliminary to effective change.'[33] With more than 'a little shooting' under way, and with no evidence of the PKI's guilt, the embassy advised British intelligence headquarters in Singapore on the line to be taken, with the aim of 'weakening the PKI permanently'.

> Suitable propaganda themes might be: PKI brutality in murdering Generals and [Foreign Minister] Nasution's daughter . . . PKI subverting Indonesia as agents of foreign Communists . . . But treatment will need to be subtle, e.g. (a) all activities should be strictly unattributable, (b) British participation or co-operation should be carefully concealed.[34]

Within two weeks, an office of the Foreign Office's Information Research Department (IRD) had opened in Singapore. The IRD was a top-secret, cold war propaganda unit headed by Norman Reddaway, one of Her Majesty's most experienced liars. It would be salutary for journalists these days to study the critical role western propaganda played then, as it does now, in shaping the news. Indeed, Reddaway and his colleagues manipulated the press so expertly that he boasted to Gilchrist in a letter marked 'secret and personal' that the story he had promoted – that Sukarno's continued rule would lead to a communist takeover – 'went all over the world and back again'. He described how an experienced Fleet Street journalist agreed 'to give exactly your angle on events in his article . . . i.e. that this was a kid glove coup without butchery.'[35]

Roland Challis, the BBC's South-East Asia correspondent, was a particular target of Reddaway, who claimed that the official version of events could be 'put almost instantly back to Indonesia via the BBC'.[36] Prevented from entering Indonesia along with other foreign journalists, Challis was unaware of the extent of the slaughter. 'It was a triumph for western propaganda,' he told me. 'My British sources purported not to know what was going on, but they knew what the American plan was. There were bodies being washed up on the lawns of the British consulate in Surabaya, and British warships escorted a ship full of Indonesian troops down the Malacca Straits so that they could take part in this terrible holocaust. It was only much later that we learned the American embassy was supplying names and ticking them off as they were killed. There was a deal, you see. In establishing the Suharto regime, the involvement of the IMF and the World Bank was part of it. Sukarno had kicked them out; now Suharto would bring them back. That was the deal.'[37]

With Sukarno now virtually powerless and ill, and Suharto about to appoint himself acting president, the American press reported the Washington-backed coup not as a great human catastrophe, but in terms of the new economic advantages. The massacres were described by *Time* as 'The West's Best News in Asia'. A headline in *US News and World Report* read: 'Indonesia: Hope . . . where there was once none'. The renowned *New York Times* columnist James Reston celebrated 'A gleam of light in Asia' and wrote a kid-glove version that he had clearly been given.[38] The Australian Prime Minister Harold Holt, who was visiting the US, offered a striking example of his sense of humour: 'With 500,000 to a million communist sympathisers knocked off,' he said approvingly, 'I think it's safe to assume a reorientation has taken place.'[39]

Holt's remark was an accurate reflection of the complicity of the

Australian foreign affairs and political establishment in the agony of its closest neighbour. The Australian embassy in Jakarta described the massacres as a 'cleansing operation'.[40] The Australian Ambassador, KCO Shann, enthused to Canberra that the Indonesian army was 'refreshingly determined to do over the PKI', adding that the generals had spoken approvingly of the reporting on Radio Australia, which he described as 'a bit dishonest'.[41] In the Prime Minister's Department, officials considered supporting 'any measures to assist the Indonesian army . . . cope with the internal situation'.[42]

In February 1966, Ambassador Gilchrist wrote a report on the scale of the massacres based on the findings of the Swedish Ambassador, who had toured central and eastern Java with his Indonesian wife and had been able to speak to people out of earshot of government officials. Gilchrist wrote to the Foreign Office: 'The Ambassador and I had discussed the killings before he left [on the tour] and he had found my suggested figure of 400,000 quite incredible. His enquiries have led him to reconsider it a very serious under-estimate. A bank manager in Surabaya with twenty employees said that four had been removed one night and beheaded . . . A third of a spinning factory's technicians, being members of a Communist union, had been killed . . . The killings in Bali had been particularly monstrous. In certain areas, it was felt that *not enough people* [emphasis in the original] had been killed.'[43]

On the island of Bali, the 'reorientation' described by Prime Minister Holt meant the violent deaths of at least 80,000 people, although this is generally regarded as a conservative figure. The many western, mostly Australian, tourists who have since taken advantage of cheap package holidays to the island might reflect that beneath the car parks of several of the major tourist hotels are buried countless bodies.

The distinguished campaigner and author Carmel Budiardjo, an Englishwoman married to a *tapol* and herself a former political prisoner, returned to Indonesia in 2000 and found 'the trauma left by the killings thirty-five years ago still gripping many communities on the island'. She described meeting, in Denpasar, fifty people who had never spoken about their experiences before in public. 'One witness,' she wrote, 'who was 20 years old at the time calmly told us how he had been arrested and held in a large cell by the military, 52 people in all, mostly members of mass organisations from nearby villages. Every few days, a batch of men was taken out, their hands tied behind their backs and driven off to be shot. Only two of the prisoners survived . . . Another witness, an ethnic Chinese Indonesian, gave testimony about the killing of 103 people, some as young as 15. In this case, the people were not arrested but simply taken from their homes and killed, as their names were ticked off a list.'[44]

In Jakarta, I went to see Heru Atmojo, an air force officer at the time of the coup and one of the thousands who, although he survived, paid dearly for his loyalty to Sukarno. He spent fifteen years in prison, much of it in solitary confinement. I should add that he is one of the most impressive individuals I have met; he reminded me of those who emerged from Robben Island, unbowed. 'I was tried by a special military tribunal,' he said. 'There were only two verdicts they handed down: a life sentence or death. I was given life, and I served fifteen years. My first cell was so small that it was almost impossible to lie down; there were just two holes for air. It was a warehouse and I was always cold. This was in Bandung in the mountains, where it is very cold, day and night. The Dutch built this jail for prisoners to be punished for twelve days. They put me there because they wanted to kill me slowly. The problem for them was that I held beliefs and principles based on reason and universal rights and these never left me in the dark confinement. You see, what happens to people like me is that although your body and health are tested, your spirit grows in the adversity. Our enemies don't understand this.'

While he was in prison, he hid his Guerrilla Star, which, under Sukarno, was Indonesia's highest honour and had been presented to him by the president himself. I asked him to wear it so that he could be photographed; and he stood, swathed in the red and white sash, with his military bearing, clipped moustache and humane eyes. His daughter, Dewi, came into the room, and they put their arms around each other. She and his other two children were ostracised as 'vermin' while he was in prison, and on his release she could barely speak to him. Now, the trauma has eased and it is clear how much she loves and admires him.

'In the early sixties,' he said, 'the pressure on Indonesia to do what the Americans wanted was intense. Sukarno wanted good relations with them, but he didn't want their economic system. With America, that is never possible. So he became an enemy. All of us who wanted an independent country, free to make our own mistakes, were made the enemy. They didn't call it globalisation then; but it was the same thing. If you accepted it, you were America's friend. If you chose another way, you were given warnings and if you didn't comply, hell was visited on you. But I am back; I am well; I have my family. They didn't win.'[45]

Ralph McGehee, a senior CIA operations officer in the 1960s, described the terror in Indonesia from 1965–66 as a 'model operation' for the American-run coup that got rid of Salvador Allende in Chile seven years later. 'The CIA forged a document purporting to reveal a leftist plot to murder Chilean military leaders,' he wrote, '[just like] what happened in Indonesia in 1965.' He says Indonesia was also the model for Operation Phoenix in Vietnam, where American-directed death squads assassinated up to 50,000 people.[46] 'You can trace back all the major, bloody events run from Washington to the way Suharto came to power,' he told me. 'The success of that meant that it would be repeated, again and again.'[47]

In November 1967, following the capture of the 'greatest prize', the booty was handed out. The Time-Life Corporation sponsored an extraordinary conference in Geneva which, in the course of three days, designed the corporate takeover of Indonesia. The participants included the most powerful capitalists in the world, the likes of David Rockefeller. All the corporate giants of the West were represented: the major oil companies and banks, General Motors, Imperial Chemical Industries, British Leyland, British-American Tobacco, American Express, Siemens, Goodyear, the International Paper Corporation, US Steel. Across the table were Suharto's men, whom Rockefeller called 'Indonesia's top economic team'.

The 'top team' was led by the Sultan of Jogjakarta, Hamengku Buwono, whom Suharto had persuaded to join him, and Adam Malik, an old political warhorse, in a triumvirate that now ruled the country. Suharto knew he needed America to underwrite him; and in April 1967, he had asked the Sultan to draw up a plan for a 'market economy'. In fact, the plan was the inspiration of the Ford Foundation, which had a long history in Indonesia, often working through CIA front organisations like the Center for International Studies, and the Stanford Research Institute, which sent a team to Jakarta immediately after the coup. It was written by Harvard economist Dave Cole, hired by the US Agency of International Development, a branch of the State Department. Cole was fresh from re-writing South Korea's banking regulations according to Washington's requirements.

In Geneva, the Sultan's team were known as the 'Berkeley Mafia', as several had enjoyed US government scholarships at the University of California in Berkeley. They came as supplicants and duly sang for their supper. Listing the principal selling points of his country and its people, the Sultan offered '. . . abundance of cheap labour . . . a treasure house of resources . . . vast potential market'.[48] Thirty-three years later, I met one of his team, Dr Emil Salim. I asked him if anyone at the Geneva conference had even mentioned that a million people had died in bringing his new business-friendly government to power. 'No, that was not on the agenda,' he replied. 'I didn't know about it till later. Remember, we didn't have television then and the telephones were not working well.'[49]

The conference was called 'To Aid in the Rebuilding of a Nation'. On the opening page of the programme was a fulsome and fictional tribute to General Suharto who, it was claimed, 'narrowly escaped being killed' in the 'communist coup'.[50] James Linen, the corpulent president of Time Inc., whose obsequious letters to Suharto had initiated the conference, opened proceedings with a prophetic description of globalisation.[51] 'We are trying to create a new climate,' he said, 'in which private enterprise and developing countries work together . . . for the greater profit of the free world. This world of international enterprise is more than governments . . . It is the seamless web of enterprise, which has been shaping the global environment at revolutionary speed.'[52]

On the second day, the Indonesian economy was carved up, sector by sector. 'This was done in a most spectacular way,' said Jeffrey Winters, professor at Northwestern University, Chicago, who, with doctoral student Brad Simpson, has studied the conference papers. 'They divided up into five different sections: mining in one room, services in another, light industry in another, banking and finance in another; and what Chase Manhattan did was sit with a delegation and hammer out policies that were going to be acceptable to them and other investors. You had these big corporate people going around the table, saying this is what we need: this, this and this, and they basically designed the legal infrastructure for investment in Indonesia. I've never heard of a situation like this where global capital sits down with the representatives of a supposedly sovereign state and hammers out the conditions of their own entry into that country.'[53]

The Freeport Company got a mountain of copper in West Papua (Henry Kissinger is currently on the board). An American and European consortium got West Papua's nickel. The giant Alcoa company got the biggest slice of Indonesia's bauxite. A group of American, Japanese and French companies got the tropical forests of Sumatra, West Papua and Kalimantan. A Foreign Investment Law, hurried on to the statutes by Suharto, made this plunder tax-free for at least five years. Real, and secret, control of the Indonesian economy passed to the Inter-Governmental Group on Indonesia (IGGI), whose principal members were the US, Canada,

Europe and Australia and, most importantly, the International Monetary Fund and the World Bank.

President Johnson wrote to James Linen, congratulating him on 'a magnificent story of opportunity seen and promise awakened'.[54] Wall Street hailed the conquest. 'The flow of American business has turned westward,' celebrated a Copley Corporation special report. 'It is [in Indonesia] that the deep-rooted American concepts of free enterprise and Yankee ingenuity are finding new forms of expression. Moreover, the profit potential fairly staggers the imagination.'[55]

Under Sukarno, Indonesia had had few debts; he had thrown out the World Bank, limited the power of the oil companies and publicly told the Americans to 'go to hell' with their loans.[56] Now the big loans rolled in, mostly from the World Bank, which had the job of tutoring the 'model pupil' on behalf of the IGGI godfathers. 'Indonesia,' said an official of the bank, 'is the best thing that's happened to Uncle Sam since World War Two.'[57]

From 1967, Indonesia was awash with World Bank dollars. In 1995, three years before Suharto's fall, James Wolfensohn, an Australian-American investment banker with close ties to the US government, took over as president of the bank. An outspoken, often truculent 'reformer', he personally attacked the few journalists who had revealed that the bank had allowed millions of dollars to pass into the pockets of the Suharto regime.

In Washington, I made an appointment to see Wolfensohn. On the morning of the interview, his assistant called me at my hotel and said, 'Mr Wolfensohn is so sorry, but he has to attend an unforeseen meeting with the Bulgarian Ambassador, sorry Danish Ambassador.'

'What's the real reason?' I asked.

'Real reason? . . . Oh hell, the *Guardian* newspaper in London is running some terrible story about Mr Wolfensohn, saying there is a civil war going on at the bank. The president is livid, he's closed his office door and says he won't speak to the media. Will you see Mr Stern instead?'

I interviewed the bank's Chief Economist, Nicholas Stern, a self-effacing former Oxford don, who had recently launched the bank's new image as an institution that 'empowered the poor'. I asked him to explain how the World Bank had 'lost' up to $10 billion in Indonesia.

'That number was plucked out of the air.'

'But the source is a World Bank report.'

'Yes, lots of times we have to guess with numbers.'

'But others corroborate it. The American Chamber of Commerce in Jakarta told me it's at least eight billion dollars.'

'Let's not get hung up on one figure . . . '

'Why not? The General Accounting of the US government looked into it and the US Senate was told that the World Bank's country director in Indonesia ignored internal reports detailing kickbacks, skimming and fraud because he was unwilling to upset the Suharto family and their cronies.'

'Okay, it's a serious question, and we have to acknowledge that we don't know how much [is missing] and it's a problem, it's a fault, we have to recognise that. But we also have to go forward . . . we're looking to support the process of decentralisation through a set of programmes which support activities at the village level: for rural roads, for clean water tanks. I visited a former leper colony which is doing brick-making and so on. So we are trying to learn from past experience and to support a country which is going through a very difficult period of adjustment.'

I asked him why, during thirty years, the World Bank had failed to say anything about a regime that was guilty of mass murder, in Indonesia and East Timor.

'I think we got a number of things wrong,' he replied, 'and we have to understand that . . .'

The apparent contrition was not a mood that survived the short walk through the tunnel that connects the World Bank and the IMF, where I met the First Deputy Managing Director, Stanley Fischer, a South African-raised economist. I asked him why the poor of Indonesia should pay the price of the misdeeds and corruption of regimes underpinned by the World Bank and the IMF.

'We're a financial institution,' he said. 'The only way we can operate is if debts are repaid . . . let me explain: you are indebted and I am indebted, and I would not be better off if I asked somebody to come and cancel my debt because I'd never be able to borrow again . . . the notion that all debt should be cancelled is a bad one.'

I said, 'The United Nations Commission on Human Rights recently reported that "the institutions of globalisation have yet to seriously address the issue of human rights. Globalisation has caused inequality and discrimination." They singled out workers in Indonesia. What's your response to that?'

'Indonesia's economy grew as a result of integrating into the global economy . . . it was a dictatorship, so people didn't have some of their human rights . . .'

'You say people didn't have some of their rights. A third of the population of East Timor died or were killed under the Suharto regime – '

'And what are you asking me that question for? Do you think we supported the Suharto regime? Don't be ridiculous!'

'Well, did you speak out against it? Did the IMF?'

'The IMF discusses the economy of countries . . .'

Indonesia, once owing nothing but having been plundered of its gold, precious stones, wood, spices and other natural riches by its colonial masters, the Dutch, today has a total indebtedness estimated at $262 billion, which is 170 per cent of its gross domestic product. There is no debt like it on earth. It can never be repaid. It is a bottomless hole.[58]

Those who will continue to repay it, at times with their lives, are the ordinary people. I met Zaenal, aged twenty-eight, his wife Ferlios, twenty-two, and their two small children, Abriyan, aged three, and Mohammed, nine months. Both infants have a rare, hereditary blood disease and must have blood transfusions once a month. Their treatment was overdue when I met the family, and it showed in their jaundiced skin and hollow eyes. Another few weeks without new blood, and they would almost certainly die. Zaenal has a job in a coat-hanger factory; half his monthly subsistence wage of £40 goes on the children's treatment and medication. They live in a labour camp on the other side of a canal from the factory. The air is still and fetid and there is the constant whine of mosquitoes. They recently sold their only electric fan; the television and telephone no longer work. The fish in the fishtank are dead. They have cut back on meat and milk and on some days they can only afford to give the children sugared tea.

What has brought them to this precipice of life or death is the soaring cost of food and fuel. Simply boiling water to make it safe costs the equivalent of £1 a day. When Stanley Fischer signed off on an IMF 'bail-out' loan to Indonesia, whose conditions include the end of subsidies on fuel, such as paraffin, and on staple foods, mainly rice, he committed Zaenal and thousands of other poor families to paying off debts incurred by a corrupt and murderous dictatorship and its cronies. As Fischer said, 'the notion that debt should be cancelled is a bad one'. At the time of writing, Zaenal's baby is in hospital, close to death.

PAYING THE PRICE

We do not seek the destruction of Iraq. Nor do we seek to punish the Iraqi people for the decisions and policies of their leaders.

President George Bush Senior

We think the price is worth it . . .
US Ambassador Madeleine Albright, when asked if the deaths of half a million Iraqi children were a price worth paying for sanctions

They know we own their country . . . we dictate the way they live and talk. And that's what's great about America right now. It's a good thing, especially when there's a lot of oil out there we need.

Brigadier-General William Looney, US air force, director of the bombing of Iraq

Wherever you go in Iraq's southern city of Basra, there is dust. It rolls down the long roads that are the desert's fingers. It gets in your eyes and nose and throat; it swirls in markets and school playgrounds, consuming children kicking a plastic ball; and it carries, according to Dr Jawad Al-Ali, 'the seeds of our death'. Dr Al-Ali is a cancer specialist at the city hospital and a member of Britain's Royal College of Physicians. He has a neat moustache and a kindly, furrowed face. His starched white coat, like the collar of his shirt, is frayed.

'Before the Gulf War, we had only three or four deaths in a month from cancer,' he said. 'Now it's thirty to thirty-five patients dying every month, and that's just in my department. That is twelve times the increase in the cancer mortality. Our studies indicate that 40 to 48 per cent of the population in this area will get cancer: in five years' time to begin with, then long afterwards. That's almost half the population. Most of my own family now have cancer, and we have no history of the disease. It has spread to the medical staff of this hospital; yesterday, the son of the medical director died. We don't know the precise source of the contamination, because we are not allowed to get the equipment to conduct a proper survey, or even test the excess level of radiation in our bodies. We strongly suspect depleted uranium, which was used by the Americans and British in the Gulf War right across the southern battlefields. Whatever the cause, it is like Chernobyl here; the genetic effects are new to us. The mushrooms grow huge, and the fish in what was once a beautiful river are inedible. Even the grapes in my garden have mutated and can't be eaten.'[1]

Along the corridor, I met Dr Ginan Ghalib Hassen, a paediatrician. At another time, she might have been described as an effervescent personality; now she, too, has a melancholy expression that does not change; it is the face of Iraq. 'This is Ali Raffa Asswadi,' she said, stopping to take the hand of a wasted boy I guessed to be about four years old. 'He is nine years,' she said. 'He has leukaemia. Now we can't treat him. Only some of the drugs are available. We get drugs for two or three weeks, and then they stop when the shipments stop. Unless you continue a course, the treatment is useless. We can't even give blood transfusions, because there are not enough blood bags . . .'

In the next bed, a child lay in his shrouded mother's arms. One side of his head was severely swollen. 'This is neuroplastoma,' said Dr Hassen. 'It is a very unusual tumour. Before 1991, we saw only one case of this tumour in two years. Now we have many cases.' Another child had his eyes fixed on me and I asked what would happen to him. She said, 'He has an abdominal mass. We have operated on him, but unless the tumour receives treatment, it will recur. We have only some drugs. We are waiting for the full course. He has renal failure now, so his future is bad. All the futures here are bad.'

Dr Hassen keeps a photo album of the children she is trying to save and has been unable to save. 'This is Talum Saleh,' she said, turning to a photograph of a boy in a blue pullover and with sparkling eyes. 'He is five-and-a-half years old. This is a case of Hodgkin's Disease. Normally, with Hodgkin's, a patient can expect to live and the cure can be 95 per cent. But if the drugs are not available, complications set in, and death follows. This boy had a beautiful nature. He died.'

I said, 'As we were walking, I noticed you stop and put your face to the wall.'

'Yes, I was emotional . . . I am a doctor; I am not supposed to cry, but I cry every day, because this is torture. These children could live; they could live and grow up; and when you see your son and daughter in front of you, dying, what happens to you?'

I said, 'What do you say to those in the West who deny the connection between depleted uranium and the deformities of these children?'

'That is not true. How much proof do they want? There is every relation between congenital malformation and depleted uranium. Before 1991, we saw nothing like this at all. If there is no connection, why have these things not happened before? Most of these children have no family history of cancer. I have studied what happened in Hiroshima. It is almost exactly the same here; we have an increased percentage of congenital malformation, an increase of malignancy, leukaemia, brain tumours: the same.'[2]

Under the economic embargo imposed by the United Nations Security Council in 1990 and upgraded the following year, Iraq is denied equipment and expertise to decontaminate its battlefields, in contrast to how Kuwait was cleaned up after the Gulf War. The US army physicist responsible for cleaning up Kuwait was Professor Doug Rokke, whom I met in London. Today, he himself is a victim. 'I am like many people in southern Iraq,' he said. 'I have 5,000 times the recommended level of radiation in my body. The contamination was right throughout Iraq and Kuwait. With the munitions testing and preparation in Saudi Arabia, uranium contamination covers the entire region. The effect depends on whether a person inhaled it or ingested it by eating and drinking, or if they got it in an open wound. What we're seeing now, respiratory problems, kidney problems, cancers, are the direct result of the use of this highly toxic material. The controversy over whether or not it's the cause is a manufactured one; my own ill-health is testament to that.'

Professor Rokke says there are two urgent issues to be confronted by people in the West, 'those with a sense of right and wrong': first, the decision by the United States and Britain to use a 'weapon of mass destruction', such as depleted uranium. He said, 'In the Gulf War, well over 300 tons were fired. An A-10 Warthog attack aircraft fired over 900,000 rounds. Each individual round was 300 grams of solid uranium 238. When a tank fired its shells, each round carried over 4,500 grams of solid uranium. These rounds are not coated, they're not tipped; they're solid uranium. Moreover, we have evidence to suggest that they were mixed with plutonium. What happened in the Gulf was a form of nuclear warfare.

'The second issue is the denial of medical care to American and British and other allied soldiers, and the tens of thousands of Iraqis contaminated. At international symposiums, I have watched Iraqi officials approach their counterparts from the Department of Defence and the Ministry of Defence and ask, plead, for help with decontamination. The Iraqis didn't use depleted uranium; it was not their weapon. They simply don't know how to get rid of it from their environment. I watched them put their case, describing the deaths and the horrific deformities that are showing up; and I watched them rebuffed. It was pathetic.'[3]

The United Nations Sanctions Committee in New York, dominated by the Americans and British, has vetoed or delayed a range of vital medical equipment, chemotherapy drugs, even pain-killers. (In the jargon of denial, 'blocked' equals vetoed, and 'on hold' means delayed, or maybe blocked.) In Baghdad, I sat in a clinic as doctors received parents and their children, many of them grey-skinned and bald, some of them dying. After every second or third examination, Dr Lekaa Fasseh Ozeer, the young oncologist, wrote in English: 'No drugs available.' I asked her to jot down in my notebook a list of drugs the hospital had ordered, but had not received, or had received intermittently. She filled a page.

I had been filming in Iraq for my documentary *Paying the Price: Killing the Children of Iraq*.[4] Back in London, I showed Dr Ozeer's list to Professor Karol Sikora who, as chief of the cancer programme of the World Health Organisation (WHO), wrote in the *British Medical Journal*: 'Requested radiotherapy equipment, chemotherapy drugs and analgesics are consistently blocked by United States and British advisers [to the Sanctions Committee]. There seems to be a rather ludicrous notion that such agents could be converted into chemical and other weapons.'[5] He told me, 'Nearly all these drugs are available in every British hospital. They're very standard. When I came back from Iraq last year, with a group of experts I drew up a list of seventeen drugs that are deemed essential for cancer treatment. We informed the UN that there was no possibility of converting these drugs into chemical warfare agents. We heard nothing more. The saddest thing I saw in Iraq was children dying because there was no chemotherapy and no pain control. It seemed crazy they couldn't have morphine, because for everybody with cancer pain, it is the best drug. When I was there, they had a little bottle of aspirin pills to go round 200 patients in pain. They would receive a particular anti-cancer drug, but then get only little bits of drugs here and there, and so you can't have any planning. It's bizarre.'

I told him that one of the doctors had been especially upset, because the UN Sanctions Committee had banned nitrous oxide as 'weapons dual use'; yet this was used in caesarean sections to stop bleeding, and perhaps save a mother's life. 'I can see no logic to banning that,' he said. 'I am not an armaments expert, but the amounts used would be so small that, even if you collected all the drugs supply for the whole nation and pooled it, it is difficult to see how you could make any chemical warfare device out of it.'

I asked him how his criticisms were received by the World Health Organisation. 'We were specifically told not to talk about it afterwards, about the whole Iraq business. The WHO was embarrassed; it's not an organisation that likes to get involved in politics.'[6]

Mohamed Ghani's studio in Baghdad is dominated by a huge crucifix he is sculpting for the Church of the Assumption in Baghdad. As Iraq's most famous sculptor, he is proud that the Vatican has commissioned him, a Muslim, to sculpt the Stations of the Cross in Rome, a cultural acknowledgement, he says, of his country as Mesopotamia, the 'cradle of western civilisation'. When I visited him, Mozart was playing on his venerable tape deck, which perched on a refrigerator of similar vintage and in which were two small bottles of beer. He handed me one. 'Here's to life and no more sorrow please,' he said. His latest work is a twenty-foot-high figure of a woman, her child gripping her legs, pleading for food. 'Every morning I see her,' he said, 'waiting, with others just like her, in a long line at the hospital at the end of my road.' He has produced a line of figurines that depict their waiting; all the heads are bowed before a door that is permanently closed. 'The door is the dispensary,' he said, 'but it is also the world, kept shut by those who rule the world.'[7]

The next day, I saw the same line of women and children at the Al Mansour children's hospital. Their doctors' anguish had a terrible echo. 'Children with meningitis can survive with the precise dosage of antibiotics,' said Dr Mohamed Mahmud. 'Four milligrams can save a life, but so often we are allowed only one milligram. This is a teaching hospital, but children die because we are not allowed parts for machines that separate blood platelets.'[8]

It was here, as we walked along the line of people waiting, that my companion Denis Halliday had an extraordinary reunion. A courtly Irishman who the previous year (1998) had resigned as the UN's Co-ordinator of Humanitarian Relief to Iraq in protest against the effects of the embargo on the civilian population, he had returned with me to Baghdad. Now he spotted a man and his daughter, and the three erupted with greetings.

'Saffa!' he said, dropping to his knees to take the hands of a nine-year-old girl.

'John, this is Saffa Majid and her father, Majid Ali. Saffa I met two years ago in this hospital, when I was the UN chief in Iraq and she was in a very poor condition with leukaemia. One cannot deal with thousands, but one can deal with two or three or four children. And I was able, with the help of the World Health Organisation, to bring in drugs, on the quiet. They were enough for two years of treatment for this little girl. And today, look at her! She looks wonderful and her father says she has only to come once a month now. So I think she's almost cured of the leukaemia. Saffa was one of four I helped. Two little girls died.'

'Why did they die?'

'They died because the medications were not available.'

'And when you set out to help these children, you were the United Nations representative here.'

'That's right. And to help them, I had to act illegally. I had to breach my own economic sanctions, so to speak, established by the Security Council, led by Washington and London. In this hospital, we have seen the evidence today of the killing that is now the responsibility of the Security Council member states, particularly Bill Clinton and Tony Blair. They should be here with us. They should see the impact of what their decisions and their sustaining of economic sanctions mean.

'The very provisions of the Charter of the United Nations and the Declaration of Human Rights are being set aside. We are waging a war, through the United Nations, on the children and people of Iraq, and with incredible results: results that you do not expect to see in a war under the Geneva Conventions. We're targeting civilians. Worse, we're targeting children like Saffa, who of course were not born when Iraq went into Kuwait. What is this about? It's a monstrous situation, for the United Nations, for the western world, for all of us who are part of some democratic system, who are in fact responsible for the policies of our governments and the implementation of economic sanctions on Iraq.'[9]

Denis Halliday had resigned after thirty-four years with the UN. He was then Assistant Secretary-General of the United Nations, with a long and distinguished career in development, 'attempting to help people, not harm them'. His was the first public expression of an unprecedented rebellion within the UN bureaucracy. 'I am resigning,' he wrote, 'because the policy of economic sanctions is totally bankrupt. We are in the process of destroying an entire society. It is as simple as that . . . Five thousand children are dying every month . . . I don't want to administer a programme that results in figures like these.'

Since I met Halliday, I have been struck by the principle behind his carefully chosen, uncompromising words. 'I had been instructed,' he said, 'to implement a policy that satisfies the definition of genocide: a deliberate policy that has effectively killed well over a million individuals, children and adults. We all know that the regime, Saddam Hussein, is not paying the price for economic sanctions; on the contrary, he has been strengthened by them. It is the little people who are losing their children or their parents for lack of untreated water. What is clear is that the Security Council is now out of control, for its actions here undermine its own Charter, and the Declaration of Human Rights and the Geneva Convention. History will slaughter those responsible.'[10]

In the UN, Halliday broke a long collective silence. On February 13, 2000, Hans Von Sponeck, who had succeeded him as Humanitarian Co-ordinator in Baghdad, resigned. Like Halliday, he had been with the UN for more than thirty years. 'How long,' he asked, 'should the civilian population of Iraq be exposed to such punishment for something they have never done?'[11] Two days later, Jutta Burghardt, head of the World Food Programme in Iraq, another UN agency, resigned, saying that she, too, could no longer tolerate what was being done to the Iraqi people.

When I met Von Sponeck in Baghdad in October 1999, the anguish behind his measured, self-effacing exterior was evident. Like Halliday's, his job had been to administer the so-called Oil for Food Programme, which since 1996 has allowed Iraq to sell a fraction of its oil for money that goes straight to an account controlled by the Security Council. Almost a third is not used on humanitarian aid, but pays the UN's 'expenses', as well as reparations demanded by Kuwait, one of the world's wealthiest nations, and compensation claims by oil companies and other multinational corporations. Iraq must then tender on the international market for food and medical supplies and other humanitarian resources. Every contract has to be approved by the UN Sanctions Committee in New York.

When sanctions were imposed, following Iraq's invasion of Kuwait in August 1990, all imports, including food, were effectively banned for eight months, even though Security Council Resolution 661 of August 6, 1990 explicitly exempted food and medicines. For a year, the UN refused to allow Iraq the means of raising funds beyond its exhausted cash reserves. As Iraq imported almost everything, the effect was immediate and devastating, compounded by the results of a bombing campaign designed to cripple the civilian infrastructure. 'US military planners,' reported the *Washington Post*, 'hoped the bombing would amplify the economic and psychological impact of international sanctions on Iraqi society . . . Because of these goals, damage to civilian structures and interests, invariably described by briefers during the war as "collateral" and unintended, was sometimes neither. The worst civilian suffering, senior officers say, has resulted not from bombs that went astray but from precision-guided weapons that hit exactly where they were aimed – at electrical plants, oil refineries and transportation networks. Among the justifications offered is that Iraqi civilians were not blameless. A senior air force officer said, "They do live there . . ." '[12]

Reporting on the aftermath of the bombing, UN Under Secretary-General Martti Ahtisaari described the 'near apocalyptic' state of the country's basic services. 'Iraq has for some time to come been relegated to a pre-industrial age,' he wrote, 'but with all the disabilities of post-industrial dependency on an intensive use of energy and technology.'[13] A Harvard University study team concluded that Iraq was heading for a 'public health catastrophe', with tens of thousands of deaths by the end of 1991 alone, the majority of them young children. The team of independent American professionals and academics estimated that, during the first eight months of sanctions when all shipments of food and medicines were blockaded, 47,000 children under the age of five had died.[14] The administration of George Bush Senior appeared to concur with these assessments;[15] and yet, wrote Dr Eric Herring of Bristol University, a sanctions specialist, 'comprehensive economic sanctions remained in place. Those policymakers who backed the sanctions cannot say that they did not know what was going to happen. Whatever the political purpose, it was a conscious and callous choice to deny an entire society the means necessary to survive.'[16]

In 1991, the Security Council, in its Resolution 687, stated that, if Iraq renounced 'weapons of mass destruction' (nuclear, biological and chemical weapons) and ballistic missiles with a range of more than 150 kilometres, and agreed to monitoring by a UN Special Commission on Iraq (UNSCOM), the embargo would be lifted.[17] In 1998, UNSCOM reported that, despite Iraqi obstruction in some areas, 'the disarmament phase of the Security Council's requirements is possibly near its end in the missile and chemical weapons areas.'[18] On December 15, 1998, the International Atomic Energy Agency reported that it had eliminated Iraq's nuclear weapons programme 'efficiently and effectively'.[19]

Scott Ritter, for five years a senior UNSCOM weapons inspector, agreed. 'By 1998, the chemical weapons infrastructure had been completely dismantled or destroyed by UNSCOM or by Iraq in compliance with our mandate,' he told me. 'The biological weapons programme was gone, all the major facilities eliminated. The nuclear weapons programme was completely eliminated. The long-range ballistic missile programme was completely eliminated. If I had to quantify Iraq's threat, I would say [it is] zero.'[20]

While food and medicines are technically exempt, the Sanctions Committee has frequently vetoed and delayed requests for baby food, agricultural equipment, heart and cancer drugs, oxygen tents, X-ray machines. Sixteen heart and lung machines were put 'on hold' because they contained computer chips. A fleet of ambulances was held up because their equipment included vacuum flasks, which keep medical supplies cold; vacuum flasks are designated 'dual use' by the Sanctions Committee, meaning they could possibly be used in weapons manufacture.[21] Cleaning materials, such as chlorine, are 'dual use', as is the graphite used in pencils; as are wheelbarrows, it seems, considering the frequency of their appearance on the list of 'holds'.[22] As of October 2001, 1,010 contracts for humanitarian supplies, worth $3.85 billion, were 'on hold' by the Sanctions Committee.[23] They included items related to food, health, water and sanitation, agriculture and education.

Most members of the Security Council want the sanctions eased considerably or lifted. The French have called them 'cruel, ineffective and dangerous'.[24] However, American dominance of the Council is such that the US and British representatives on the Sanctions Committee alone veto and delay contracts. The British claim they hold up only 'one per cent' of humanitarian contracts.[25] This is sophistry; by never objecting to American obstruction, they give it tacit support. Moreover, a veto or 'hold' can only be rescinded by the Council member who orders it.

So blatant is the obstruction that Kofi Annan, the UN Secretary-General virtually appointed by the Americans, complained that the delays and vetoes were 'seriously impairing the effective implementation of the [Oil for Food] programme'. He urged the approval of water, sanitation and electricity contracts 'without delay' because of 'their paramount importance to the welfare of the Iraqi people'.[26] The Executive Director of the UN Office of the Iraq Programme, Benon Sevan, has attacked the Council for holding up spares for Iraq's crumbling oil industry, warning that the less oil Iraq is able to pump, the less money will be available to buy food and medicine.[27] In 1999, a senior Clinton administration official told the *Washington Post*, 'The longer we can fool around in the [Security] Council and keep things static, the better.'[28]

In Britain, Customs and Excise have stopped parcels going to Iraqi relatives, containing children's clothes and toys. The chairman of the British Library, John Ashworth, wrote to Harry Cohen MP that, 'after consultation with the Foreign Office', it was decided that books could no longer be sent to Iraqi students.[29] The British Library had already distinguished itself by informing a translator in Baghdad that it was not permitted to send him a copy of James Joyce's *Ulysses*. From the petty and craven to the farcical: an attempt to send documents to Iraq advising Iraqis on human rights and press freedom was blocked by the Department of Trade and Industry in London. The package, which also contained advice on family planning and Aids, was posted to Mosul University but was intercepted and returned to Article 19, the anti-censorship group.[30]

When Denis Halliday was the senior United Nations official in Iraq, a display cabinet stood in the foyer of his office. It contained a bag of wheat, some congealed cooking oil, bars of soap and a few other household necessities. 'It was a pitiful sight,' he said, 'and it represented the monthly ration that we were allowed to spend. I added cheese to lift the protein content, but there was simply not enough money left over from the amount we were allowed to spend, which came from the revenue Iraq was allowed to make from its oil.'[31] He describes food shipments as 'an exercise in duplicity'. A shipment that the Americans claim allows for 2,300 calories per person per day may well allow for only 2,000 calories, or fewer. 'What's missing,' he said, 'will be animal proteins, minerals and vitamins. As most Iraqis have no other source of income, food has become a medium of exchange; it gets sold for other necessities, further lowering the calorie intake. You also have to get clothes and shoes for your kids to go to school. You've then got malnourished mothers who cannot breastfeed, and they pick up bad water. What is needed is investment in water treatment and distribution, electric power production for food processing, storage and refrigeration, education and agriculture.'[32]

His successor, Hans Von Sponeck, calculates that the Oil for Food Programme allows $100 for each person to live on for a year. This figure also has to help pay for the entire society's infrastructure and essential services, such as power and water. 'It is simply not possible to live on such an amount,' Von Sponeck told me. 'Set that pittance against the lack of clean water, the fact that electricity fails for up to twenty-two hours a day, and the majority of sick people cannot afford treatment, and the sheer trauma of trying to get from day to day, and you have a glimpse of the nightmare. And make no mistake, this is deliberate. I have not in the past wanted to use the word genocide, but now it is unavoidable.'[33]

The cost in lives is staggering. A study by the United Nations Children's Fund, Unicef, found that between 1991 and 1998, there were 500,000 deaths above the anticipated rate among Iraqi children under five years of age. This, on average, is 5,200 preventable under-five deaths per month.[34] Hans Von Sponeck said, 'Some 167 Iraqi children are dying every day.'[35] Denis Halliday said, 'If you include adults, the figure is now almost certainly well over a million.'[36]

In 1999, a humanitarian panel set up by the Security Council reported that Iraq had slipped from 'relative affluence' prior to 1991 into 'massive poverty'. The panel criticised the Oil for Food Programme as 'inadequate' to remedy a 'dire' humanitarian situation 'that cannot be overstated'. The panel's members took the remarkable step of attacking their sponsor, charging that 'the Iraqi people would not be undergoing such deprivations in the absence of the prolonged measures imposed by the Security Council'. Once again, children were found to be the main victims, with the infant mortality rate soaring from one of the lowest in the world in 1990 to the highest.[37]

In a separate study, Richard Garfield, a renowned epidemiologist at Columbia University in New York, says that, in tripling since 1990, the death rate of children in Iraq is unique. 'There is almost no documented case,' he wrote, 'of rising mortality for children under five years in the modern world'.[38] Extrapolating from these statistics, American researchers John Mueller and Karl Mueller conclude that 'economic sanctions have probably already taken the lives of more people in Iraq than have been killed by all weapons of mass destruction in history.'[39]

In 1999, seventy members of the US Congress signed an unusually blunt letter to President Clinton, appealing to him to lift the embargo and end what they called 'infanticide masquerading as policy'.[40] The Clinton administration had already given them their reply. In 1996, in an infamous interview on the American current affairs programme *60 Minutes*, Madeleine Albright, then US

Ambassador to the United Nations, had been asked: 'We have heard that half a million children have died . . . is the price worth it?' Albright replied, 'I think this is a very hard choice, but the price – we think the price is worth it.'[41]

My journey to Iraq was almost surreal. With Denis Halliday and my television colleagues Alan Lowery, Preston Clothier and Grant Roberts, I spent sixteen anxious hours on a road that is a ribbon of wreckage. Pieces of tyre drifted towards us, like giant black birds escaping the squalls of sand and dust. Beside the road lay two bodies. They were old men in suits, as if laid out for their funeral, their arms stiffly by their sides. A taxi rested upside-down. The men had been walking to the border, each with his meagre belongings, now scattered among the thornbushes. The taxi's brakes had apparently failed and it had cut them down. Local people came out of the dust and stood beside the bodies: for them, on this, the only road in and out of Iraq, it was a common sight.

The road from Amman in Jordan to Baghdad was never meant as an artery, yet it now carries most of Iraq's permissible trade and traffic to the outside world. Two narrow single lanes are dominated by oil tankers, moving in an endless convoy; cars and overladen buses and vans dart in and out in a *danse macabre*. The inevitable carnage provides a roadside tableau of burnt-out tankers, a bus crushed like a tin can, an official United Nations Mercedes on its side, its once-privileged occupants dead. Of course, brakes fail on rickety taxis everywhere, but the odds against survival here are greatly shortened. Parts for the older

models are now non-existent, and drivers go through the night
and day with little sleep. With the Iraqi dinar worth virtually
nothing, they must go back and forth, from Baghdad to Amman,
Amman to Baghdad, as frequently and as quickly as possible. And
when they and their passengers are killed or maimed, they, too,
become victims of the most ruthless economic embargo of
modern times.

Baghdad was just visible beneath a white pall of pollution.
Young arms reached up to the window of our van: a boy offering
an over-ripe banana, a girl a single stem flower. Before 1990,
begging was almost unknown and frowned upon. Baghdad today
is an urban version of Rachel Carson's *Silent Spring*. The birds have
gone as avenues of palms have died, in what was once the land of
dates. The splashes of colour, on fruit stalls, are three-dimensional. A bunch of Dole bananas and a bag of apples from Beirut
cost a teacher's salary for a month; only foreigners and the rich eat
fruit.

The rich, the black marketeers, the regime's cronies and
favoured supplicants, are not visible, except for an occasional
tinted-glass late-model Mercedes navigating its way through the
rustbuckets. Having been ordered to keep their heads down, the
elite keep to their network of clubs and restaurants and well-
stocked clinics, the presence of which make nonsense of claims in
Washington and London that the sanctions are hurting the
regime.

The Al Rasheed Hotel is where Saddam Hussein's people are
glimpsed. Dark glasses, large dyed moustaches and spooks prolif-
erate. You enter by way of an icon of dark Iraqi humour, crossing
a large floor portrait, set in tiles, of George Bush Senior, a good
likeness, and the words: 'George Bush is a war criminal'. The face

is forever being polished. I met an assistant manager, who had been at the hotel since the 1980s and whose sardonic sense of western double standards was a treat. 'Ah, a journalist from Britain!' he said. 'Would you like to see where Mr Douglas Hurd stayed, and Mr David Melon [sic] and Mr Tony Newton, and all the other members of Mrs Thatcher's Government . . . These gentlemen were our friends, our *benefactors*.' He has a collection of the *Baghdad Observer* from 'the good old days'. Saddam Hussein is on the front page, where he always is. The only change in each photograph is that he is sitting on his white presidential couch with a different British government minister, who is smiling or wincing.

There is Douglas Hurd, in 1981, then a Foreign Office minister who came to sell Saddam Hussein a British Aerospace missile system and to 'celebrate' the anniversary of the coming to power of the Ba'ath (Redemption) Party, a largely CIA triumph in 1968 that extinguished all hope of a pluralistic Iraq and produced Saddam Hussein. There is Hurd twice: on the couch and on page two, bowing before the tyrant, the renowned interrogator and torturer of Qasr-al-Nihayyah, the 'palace of the end'. And there is the corpulent David Mellor, also a Foreign Office man, on the same white couch in 1988. While Mellor, or 'Mr Melon' as the assistant manager preferred, was being entertained, his host ordered the gassing of 5,000 Kurds in the town of Halabja, news of which the Foreign Office tried to suppress.[42] And there is Tony Newton, Margaret Thatcher's Trade Secretary, who, within a month of the gassing of the Kurds, was on the same white couch offering Saddam £340 million of British tax-payers' money in export credits. And there he is again, three months later, back on the couch, celebrating the fact that Iraq was now Britain's third-largest market for machine tools, from which a range of weapons was forged. As the subsequent inquiry by Sir Richard Scott revealed, these celebrities of the *Baghdad Observer* knew they were dealing illegally with the tyrant. 'Please give Mr Melon my greetings,' said the assistant manager.

Read carefully, history will usually offer an explanation. A few miles from the Al Rasheed is a cemetery girded by iron railings, behind which lines of stone crosses are just visible through drifting skeins of dust and sand. This is the British Cemetery, where soldiers who fought the Turks near the end of the First World War are buried. 'Here have been recovered or interred,' says a plaque, 'the bodies of British officers and men who, after the fall of Kut, being prisoners in the hands of the Turks, perished . . . These are they who came out of great tribulation.' Private FR Reynolds of the Imperial Camel Corps was nineteen when he was killed on October 11, 1918. His cross has crumbled. Frederic Ivor Hesiger, Second Lieutenant Royal Field Artillery, was twenty when he was mortally wounded at the battle of Shatt-Eladhaim on April 30, 1917. Being the eldest son of the Third Baron Chelmsford, Viceroy of India, he has his own tomb, which weeds and vines have claimed. None of the inscriptions says: 'He died to secure a stupendous source of strategic power, and one of the greatest material prizes in world history'. That was how the US State Department in 1945 described the oilfields of the Middle East.[43]

After oil was discovered in the late nineteenth century, the European powers lost no time in getting their hands on 'the greatest prize'. By 1918, they had seen off the Ottoman Turks and divided up their empire. Iraq and all the Arab lands became colonies, despite earlier promises of independence after the war. France kept Syria, Lebanon and northern Iraq; Britain seized

Baghdad and Basra in the south. The long-suffering Kurds were kept in a separate region under the British; and when they rose up, Winston Churchill, the Colonial Secretary, mused: 'I do not understand this squeamishness about the use of gas. I am strongly in favour of using poisoned gas against uncivilised tribes.'

Having crowned a puppet Iraqi king, Faisal, the British set about destroying the independence movement by pulverising villages with artillery and bombing farmlands with phosphorus bombs and metal crowsfeet designed to maim livestock. Iraq, source of the world's highest-grade oil, remained a British colony in all but name until the Suez invasion in 1956.

Two years later, the Iraqi monarchy was overthrown by a nationalist, Abd al-Karim Kassem, who himself fell victim to an internecine struggle. The new regime called itself an 'Arab socialist union', and a measure of plurality included a decentralised administration and recognition of the Kurdish language and national identity. When the Iraq Petroleum Company, the foreign consortium that exploited Iraq's oil, was threatened with nationalisation in 1963, the new imperial power, the United States, engineered what the Central Intelligence Agency called its 'favourite coup'. 'We regarded it as a great victory,' said James Critchfield, then head of the CIA in the Middle East.[44] The Secretary-General of the Ba'ath Party, Ali Saleh Sa'adi, concurred. 'We came to power on a CIA train,' he said, thereafter instigating a reign of terror that produced Saddam Hussein, who became the top man in 1979. He was America's man. 'Saddam has a great deal to thank the CIA for,' Said Aburish, his biographer, told me. 'He can thank them for bringing the Ba'ath Party to power, for helping him personally, for providing him with financial aid during the war with Iran, for protecting him against internal coups d'état. It's a continuing relationship from the early 1960s until now, and it's a love/hate relationship.'[45]

So enduring was America's ardour, or rather its gratitude to Iraq for protecting its client Arab states from Iran's revolutionary virus, that Saddam Hussein was given everything he wanted, almost up to the day he invaded Kuwait in August 1990. When John Kelly, the US Assistant Secretary of State, visited Baghdad in 1989, he told him: 'You are a force for moderation in the region, and the United States wants to broaden her relationship with Iraq.'[46] The 'force for moderation' had just claimed victory in a war against Iran, which resulted in more than a million casualties on both sides, dead and wounded. When human rights groups presented evidence that Saddam Hussein had used mustard gas and nerve gas against Iranian soldiers and Kurdish civilians, the State Department refused to condemn him.[47] As Saddam Hussein was preparing his forces for the attack on his southern neighbour, a US Department of Energy official discovered that advanced nuclear reactors were being shipped to Iraq. When he alerted his superiors, he was moved to another job. 'We knew about their bomb programme,' said a former member of the Bush administration, 'but Saddam was our ally . . .'[48]

In 1992, a Congressional inquiry found that President George Bush Senior and his top advisers had ordered a cover-up to conceal their secret support for Saddam Hussein and the illegal arms shipments being sent to him via third countries. Missile technology was shipped to South Africa and Chile and then 'on sold' to Iraq, while Commerce Department records were altered and deleted. (This mirrored the emerging scandal across the Atlantic, which saw British weapons technology being illegally shipped to Iraq, with Jordan listed on the 'end-user' certificates.) Within weeks of the

Iraqi invasion of Kuwait, the CIA was still feeding copious intelligence to Baghdad. Congressman Henry Gonzalez, chairman of the House of Representatives banking committee, said, 'Bush and his advisers financed, equipped and succoured the monster they later set out to slay, and they were now burying the evidence.'[49]

A 1994 Senate report documented the transfer to Iraq of the ingredients of biological weapons: botulism developed at a company in Maryland, licensed by the Commerce Department and approved by the State Department.[50] Anthrax was also supplied by the Porton Down laboratories in Britain, a government establishment.[51] A Congressional investigator said, 'It was all money, it was all greed. The US Government knew, the British Government knew. Did they care? No. It was a competition with the Germans. That's how the arms trade works.'[52]

During the parallel Scott Inquiry in London into the arms-to-Iraq scandal, Tim Laxton, a City of London auditor, was brought in to examine the books of the British arms company Astra, which the Thatcher Government covertly and illegally used as a channel for arms to Iraq. Laxton was one of the few observers to sit through the entire inquiry. He believes that if Sir Richard Scott's brief had been open and unlimited, and Thatcher's senior aides and civil servants had been compelled to give evidence under oath, as well as numerous other vital witnesses who were not called, the outcome would have been very different from the temporary embarrassment meted out to a few ministers. 'Hundreds,' he said, 'would have faced criminal investigation, including top political figures, very senior civil servants from the Foreign Office, the Ministry of Defence, the Department of Trade . . . the top echelon of government.'[53]

In the centre of Baghdad is a monolith that crowds the eye; it commemorates, or celebrates, the 1980–90 Iran–Iraq war, which Saddam Hussein started, urged on by the Americans who wanted him to destroy their new foe in the region, the Ayatollah Khomeini. Cast in a foundry in Basingstoke, its two huge forearms, reputedly modelled on Saddam Hussein's own, hold triumphant crossed sabres. Cars are allowed to drive over the helmets of dead Iranian soldiers embedded in the concourse. I cannot think of a sight anywhere in the world that better expresses the crime of sacrificial war and the business of making and selling armaments: America and Britain supplied both sides with weapons.

We stayed at the Hotel Palestine, a far cry from the Al Rasheed. The smell of petrol is constant; if you stay too long inside, you feel sick. With contracts for disinfectant 'on hold' in New York, petrol, more plentiful than water, has replaced it. In the lobby there is an Iraqi Airways office, which is open every day, with an employee sitting behind a desk, smiling and saying good morning to passing guests. She has no clients, because there is no Iraqi Airways, which died with sanctions. Two of the pilots are outside, waiting beside their empty taxis; others are sweeping the forecourt or selling used clothes.

In my room, the plaster crumbled every night and the water ran gravy brown. The one frayed towel was borne by the maid like an heirloom. When I asked for coffee to be brought up, the waiter hovered outside until I was finished; cups are at a premium. 'I am always sad,' he said matter-of-factly. In a month, he will have earned enough to pay for somebody to go to Amman to buy tablets for his brother's epilepsy.

A melancholia shrouds people. I felt it at Baghdad's evening auctions, where intimate possessions are sold in order to buy food and medicines. Television sets are common items up for sale. A woman with two infants watched their pushchairs go for pennies. A man who had collected doves since he was fifteen came with his last bird; the cage would go next. My film crew and I had come to pry, yet we were made welcome; or people merely deferred to our presence, as the downcast do. During three weeks in Iraq, only once was I the brunt of someone's anguish. 'Why are you killing the children?' shouted a man in the street. 'Why are you bombing us? What have we done to you?' Passers-by moved quickly to calm him; one of them placed an affectionate arm on his shoulder, another, a teacher, materialised at my side. 'We do not connect the people of Britain with the actions of the government,' he said, reassuringly. Those Muslims in Britain, terrified to leave their homes after the bombing of Afghanistan, have little of the personal security I felt in Iraq.

Through the glass doors of the offices of Unicef, the United Nations Children's Fund in Baghdad, you can read the following mission statement: 'Above all, survival, hope, development, respect, dignity, equality and justice for women and children.' Fortunately, the children in the street outside, with their pencil limbs and long thin faces, cannot read English, and perhaps cannot read at all. 'The change in such a short time is unparalleled, in my experience,' Dr Anupama Rao Singh, Unicef's senior representative in Iraq, told me. 'In 1989, the literacy rate was more than 90 per cent; parents were fined for failing to send their children to school. The phenomenon of street children was unheard of. Iraq had reached a stage where the basic indicators we use to measure the overall wellbeing of human beings, including children, were some of the best in the world. Now it is among the bottom 20 per cent.'

Dr Singh, diminutive, grey-haired and, with her preciseness, sounding like the teacher she once was in India, has spent most of her working life with Unicef. Helping children is her vocation, but now, in charge of a humanitarian programme that can never succeed, she says, 'I am grieving.'

She took me to a typical primary school in Saddam City, where Baghdad's majority and poorest live. We approached along a flooded street, the city's drainage and water distribution system having collapsed since the Gulf War bombing. The headmaster, Ali Hassoon, guided us around the puddles of raw sewage in the playground and pointed to the high-water mark on the wall. 'In the winter it comes up to here. That's when we evacuate. We stay for as long as possible but, without desks, the children have to sit on bricks. I am worried about the buildings coming down.' As we talked, an air-raid siren sounded in the distance.

The school is on the edge of a vast industrial cemetery. The pumps in the sewage treatment plants and the reservoirs of potable water are silent, save for a few wheezing at a fraction of their capacity. Those that were not bombed have since disintegrated; spare parts from their British, French and German manufacturers are permanently 'on hold'. Before 1991, Baghdad's water was as safe as any in the developed world. Today, drawn untreated from the Tigris, it is lethal. Touching two brothers on the head, the headmaster said, 'These children are recovering from dysentery, but it will attack them again, and again, until they are too weak.' Dr Singh told me that, in 1990, an Iraqi child with dysentery, or other water-borne illness, stood a one-in-600 chance of dying; today, it is up to one in fifty.[54]

Just before Christmas 1999, the Department of Trade and Industry in London restricted the export of vaccines meant to protect Iraqi children against diphtheria and yellow fever. Dr Kim Howells told Parliament why. His title of Parliamentary Under-Secretary of State for Competition and Consumer Affairs perfectly suited his Orwellian reply. The children's vaccines were, he said, 'capable of being used in weapons of mass destruction'.[55]

'Much of the suffering is unseen,' said Dr Singh. 'There has been a 125 per cent increase in children seeking help for mental health problems. In a society that takes education very seriously, most homes have been denuded of the very basic stimulation materials, books and toys, because most families, in order to cope, have sold everything except the bare essentials. We have here a whole generation who have grown up with a sense of total isolation and a feeling of dependency, and the lack of hope. I often think of my own nieces and nephews, and I ask myself, "Would I accept this for my own family?" and, if I wouldn't, then it's unacceptable for the children of Iraq. This is not an empty emotion. It's a fundamental tenet of the [UN] Convention of the Rights of the Child: Article Two, the Principle of Non-Discrimination. It is simply their right not to lose out in terms of their life.'

In an Edwardian colonnade of Doric and Corinthian columns, schoolchildren and college students come to sell their books, not as in a flea market, but out of urgent need. Teachers and other professionals part with treasured history volumes and art books, leather-bound in Baghdad in the 1930s, obstetrics and radiology texts, copies of the *British Medical Journal*, first and second editions of *Waiting for Godot*, *The Sun Also Rises* and, no less, *British Housing Policy 1958*. A man with a clipped grey moustache, an Iraqi Bertie Wooster, said, 'I need to go south to see my sister, who is ill. Please be kind and give me twenty-five dinars [about a penny].' He took it, nodded and walked smartly away. A teacher said, 'You know, I have sold every book I own, including my Koran and my dictionary.' A nineteen-year-old engineering student said, 'I just sold my pens. I have one left.'

Felicity Arbuthnot and I spotted a book called *Peace Flows from the Sky*. We stared at such bleakly ironic words, and bought it. Such is the terrible plight of this society that even a collection of almost childishly sentimental poetry had the power to stir:

> Peace flows
> from the sky
> through the air
> to me . . .
> The birds' singing
> brings me out of my trance
> to remind me of life . . .

Felicity has spent the past decade alerting the outside world to the suffering of the Iraqi people. Time and again, she has braved the terrible road from Amman, never complaining about her personal hardship, always inspired by the courage of Iraqis she has befriended, especially children. (Read her tribute to and obituary of Jassim, 'The Little Poet', *New Internationalist*, November 1998.) When I set out from Jordan with Felicity and Denis Halliday (both are Irish), she nursed a broken wrist in a sling. Every pothole brought agony, which she disguised with cheerfulness. She reminds me of another humanitarian journalist and adventurer, Martha Gellhorn: she drinks, laughs, gets incensed at injustice and hypocrisy, cares about the powerless, and writes beautifully; and she once drove a red Alfa Romeo ('It had a walnut dashboard') all the way from Miami to Mexico City.[56]

I had asked Felicity to do research for the filming of my documentary, *Paying the Price*. We drove to the northern city of Mosul, through a moonscape evocative of Monument Valley in California. We arrived at what had been a scene of devastation six months earlier, when Felicity had been here. On the dusty open ground there were still pieces of a water tanker, shrapnel from a missile, a shoe, and the wool and remains of sheep. 'I found this whole area strewn with dead sheep,' she said. 'There were the bodies of two sheepdogs, and personal belongings. It was clearly blast damage. The tanker was riddled with bullet holes. Local people told me it happened on a Friday, the Sabbath, and so the villagers had all come down, and about forty to fifty were sharing an early-morning meal. When they went back, they left the family of six, the grandfather, the father and four children, to mind the sheep. They heard the plane and the bombs drop. They came running back. They said they searched from early morning until dark to try to find the bodies to bury them within twelve hours, in accordance with Islam.'[57]

We found the brother of the shepherd, Hussain Jarsis. He agreed to meet us at the cemetery where his father, brother and the four children are buried. He arrived in an old Toyota van with the shepherd's widow, whose name is Icdai Thanoon. She was hunched with grief, her face covered. She held the hand of her one remaining child, and they sat beside the mounds of earth on the children's graves and she wept. When Felicity went over to her to apologise for the atrocity, the figure in black stood up, faced her and said, 'I want to speak to the pilot who killed my four children.'

Her husband's brother is also a shepherd. After he had prayed at the gravesides, he said. 'When I arrived to look for my brother and family, the planes were circling overhead. I hadn't reached the causeway when the fourth bombardment took place. The last two rockets hit them. At the time I couldn't grasp what was going on. The truck was burning. It was a big truck, but it was ripped to pieces. Nothing remained except the numberplate and the tyres you saw. We saw three corpses, but the rest were just body parts. And the sheep. With the last rocket, I could see the sheep blasted into the air. The rocket burned an area of a hundred square metres: total incineration. In the last bombardment, the planes were very low. That's when they fired two rockets simultaneously. There were six dead people: my father, who was seventy years old, my brother, who was thirty-five, along with his four children. The youngest was Sultan, who was five. He hadn't been accepted into school yet. He told me, "Uncle, they'll take me next year." God Almighty didn't let him do it. We belong to God and to Him we shall return.'[58]

Without livestock, the family is penniless. I offered him money. He declined, but asked me if I would come to his home for something to eat.

The attack was investigated, and verified, by Hans Von Sponeck, the senior UN official in Iraq, who drove there especially from Baghdad. Nothing nearby resembled a military installation. The valley is treeless, open and desolate. Von Sponeck recorded his finding in a confidential internal document, *Air Strikes in Iraq: 28 December 1998–31 May 1999*, prepared by the UN Security Section (UNOHCI). Dozens of similar attacks were described: on villages, a fishermen's wharf, near a World Food Programme warehouse. He ordered UN relief convoys suspended for several hours in the afternoon, when many of the attacks occurred.

When she returned to London after seeing the evidence of the atrocity, Felicity had phoned the Ministry of Defence. 'I've just come back from Mosul,' she said, 'and you are bombing sheep, and I wondered if you have a comment.'

The official replied, 'We reserve the right to take robust action if threatened.'[59]

We drove into the dung-coloured hills beyond Mosul, along a precarious road to a fourth-century monastery that commands the valleys. St Matthew is buried here and Iraqi Christians come in their hundreds to pray at his shrine. At weekends, the monastery is a popular place to picnic; I met a family of twenty: the youngest two years old, the eldest eighty-six. They had relatives in Australia and I took their photograph, and later sent copies to them in Mosul and the Australian branch in suburban Sydney. They talked about the bombing, shaking their heads and holding the young children close to them. 'Why?' they asked. A priest said, 'The safety and peace these people felt here has been taken away. Last year, dozens of people climbed the slopes to watch the eclipse of the sun – it was one of the clearest views anywhere in the world – and the planes came and bombed: American or British, I don't know. Five people were killed, we were told. Every day, we hear the thump-thump. What are they attacking?'

American and British aircraft operate over Iraq in what their governments have unilaterally declared 'no fly zones'. This means that only they and their allies can fly there. The designated areas are in the north, around Mosul, to the border with Turkey, and from just south of Baghdad to the Kuwaiti border. The US and British governments insist the no fly zones are 'legal', claiming that they are part of, or supported by, the Security Council's Resolution 688.

There is a great deal of fog about this, the kind generated by the Foreign Office when its statements are challenged. There is no reference to no fly zones in Security Council resolutions, which suggests they have no basis in international law. To be sure about this, I went to Paris and asked Dr Boutros Boutros-Ghali, the Secretary-General of the UN in 1992, when the resolution was passed. 'The issue of no fly zones was not raised and therefore not debated: not a word,' he said. 'They offer no legitimacy to countries sending their aircraft to attack Iraq.'

'Does that mean they are illegal?' I asked.

'They are illegal,' he replied.

The scale of the bombing in the no fly zones is astonishing. During the eighteen months to January 14, 1999, American air force and naval aircraft flew 36,000 sorties over Iraq, including 24,000 combat missions.[60] During 1999, American and British aircraft dropped more than 1,800 bombs and hit 450 targets.[61] The cost to British taxpayers is more than £800 million.[62] There is bombing almost every day: it is the longest Anglo-American aerial campaign since the Second World War; yet it is mostly ignored by the British and American media. In a rare acknowledgement, the *New York Times* reported, 'American warplanes have methodically and with virtually no public discussion been attacking Iraq . . . pilots have flown about two-thirds as many missions as Nato pilots flew over Yugoslavia in seventy-eight days of around-the-clock war there.'[63]

The purpose of the no fly zones, according to the British and American governments, is to protect the Kurds in the north and the Shi'a in the south against Saddam Hussein's forces. The aircraft are performing a 'vital humanitarian task', says Tony Blair, that will give 'minority peoples the hope of freedom and the right to determine their own destinies'.

Blair's specious words are given the lie by a secret history. When Saddam Hussein was driven from Kuwait, in 1991, his generals were surprised to be told by the victors that they could keep their helicopter gunships. The British commander, General Sir Peter de la Billière, defended this decision with the following astonishing logic: 'The Iraqis were responsible for establishing law and order. You could not administer the country without using the helicopters.'[64] Law and order? The same law and order that approved the gassing of 5,000 Kurds at Halabja? A clue was given in a chance remark by Prime Minister John Major. 'I don't recall,' said Major, 'asking the Kurds to mount this particular insurrection . . .'[65]

Turkey is critical to the American 'world order'. Overseeing the oilfields of the Middle East and former Soviet Central Asia, it is a member of Nato and the recipient of billions of dollars' worth of American arms. It is where American and British fighter-bombers are based. A long-running insurrection by Turkish Kurds, led by the Kurdish Workers' Party (PKK), is regarded by Washington as a threat to the 'stability' of Turkey's crypto-fascist regime. Following the Gulf War, the last thing the Americans wanted was tens of thousands of Iraqi Kurds arriving in Turkey as refugees and boosting the struggle of local Kurds against the regime in Ankara. Their anxieties were reflected in Security Council Resolution 688, which warned of a 'massive flow of refugees towards and across international frontiers . . . which threatens international peace and security in the region . . .'

What the refugees threatened was Turkey's capacity to continue to deny basic human rights to the Kurds within its borders. The northern no fly zone offered a solution. Since 1992, the zones have provided cover for Turkey's repeated invasions of Iraq. In 1995 and 1997, as many as 50,000 Turkish troops, backed by tanks, fighter-bombers and helicopter gunships, occupied swathes of the Kurds' 'safe haven', allegedly attacking PKK bases. In December 2000, they were back, terrorising Kurdish villages and murdering civilians. The US and Britain said nothing; the Security Council said nothing. Moreover, the British and Americans colluded in the invasions, suspending their flights to allow the Turks to get on with the killing. Virtually none of this was reported in the western media.

In March 2001, RAF pilots patrolling the northern no fly zone publicly protested for the first time about their role in the bombing of Iraq. Far from performing the 'vital humanitarian task' described by Tony Blair, they complained that they were frequently ordered to return to their Turkish base to allow the Turkish air force to bomb the Kurds in Iraq, the very people they were meant to be 'protecting'. Speaking on a non-attributable basis to Dr Eric Herring, the Iraqi sanctions specialist at Bristol University, they said that whenever the Turks wanted to bomb the Kurds in Iraq, the RAF aircraft were recalled to base and ground crews were told to switch off their radar so that the Turks' targets would not be visible. One British pilot reported seeing the devastation in Kurdish villages caused by the attacks when he resumed his patrol. 'They were very unhappy about what they had been ordered to do and what they had seen,' said Dr Herring, 'especially as there had been no official explanation.'[66]

In October 2000, the *Washington Post* reported: 'On more than one occasion [US pilots who fly in tandem with the British] have received a radio message that "there is a TSM inbound": that is, a "Turkish Special Mission" heading into Iraq. Following standard orders, the Americans turned their planes around and flew back to Turkey. "You'd see Turkish F-14s and F-16s inbound, loaded to the gills with munitions," [pilot Mike Horn] said. "Then they'd come out half an hour later with their munitions expended." When the Americans flew back into Iraqi air space, he recalled, they would see "burning villages, lots of smoke and fire".[67]

During the Gulf War, President George Bush Senior called on 'the Iraqi military and the Iraqi people to take matters into their hands and force Saddam Hussein to step aside'. [68] In March 1991, the majority Shi'a people in the south rallied to Bush's call and rose up. So successful were they, at first, that within two days Saddam Hussein's rule had collapsed across southern Iraq and the popular uprising had spread to the country's second city, Basra. A new start for the people of Iraq seemed close at hand. Then the tyrant's old paramour in Washington intervened just in time.

'The opposition,' Said Aburish told me, 'found themselves confronted with the United States helping Saddam Hussein against them. The Americans actually stopped rebels from reaching arms depots. They denied them shelter. They gave Saddam Hussein's Republican Guard safe passage through American lines in order to attack the rebels. They did everything except join the fight on his side.'[69] In their book, *Out of the Ashes: the Resurrection of Saddam Hussein*, Andrew and Patrick Cockburn describe the anguish of one of the rebel leaders, a brigadier, who watched American helicopters circling overhead as Iraqi government helicopter crews poured kerosene on columns of fleeing refugees and set them alight with tracer fire. 'I saw with my own eyes the American planes flying over the helicopters,' he said. 'We were expecting them to help; now we could see them witnessing our demise . . . They were taking pictures and they knew exactly what was happening.'[70] In Nasiriyah, American troops prevented the rebels from taking guns and ammunition from the army barracks. 'The Iraqis explained to the American commander who they were and why they were there,' wrote the Cockburns. 'It was not a warm reception . . . The US officer went away for ten minutes and then returned with the curious claim that he was out of touch with his headquarters. [He] curtly suggested that they try and find the French forces, eighty miles to the west.'

The rebels eventually found a French colonel, who wanted to help; but when he tried to set up a meeting with General Schwarzkopf, the American commander, he was told this was not possible. The revolt was doomed; crucial time had been lost. The first city to fall to Saddam Hussein was Basra. Tanks captured the main road and demolished the centres of resistance. 'It was a bad time,' said a doctor at the hospital. 'You could see dogs eating bodies in the streets.'[71]

In the north, the Kurds, too, had risen up: the revolt John Major said he had 'never asked for'. Saddam Hussein's Republican Guards, who had been pointedly spared by Schwarzkopf, entered the Kurdish town of Sulaimaniya and extinguished the Kurdish resistance. Saddam Hussein had survived by a whisker; as his troops were celebrating their victory, their ammunition ran out.[72] Five years later, when Saddam Hussein sent his tanks into another rebellious Kurdish town, Arbil, American aircraft circled the city for twenty minutes, then flew away. The CIA contingent among the Kurds managed to flee to safety, while ninety-six members of the CIA-funded Iraqi National Congress were rounded up and executed.[73] According to Ahmed Chalabi of the INC, tacit American support for the regime was 'the most significant factor in the suppression of the uprising. They made it possible for Saddam to regroup his forces and launch a devastating counterattack with massive firepower on the people.'[74]

Why? What the Americans fear is that the Kurds might establish their own state, perhaps even socialist and democratic, and that the Shi'a might forge an 'Islamic alliance' with Iran. What they do not want is for them to 'take matters into their own hands'. The American television journalist Peter Jennings put it this way: 'The United States did not want Saddam Hussein to go, they just didn't want the Iraqi people to take over.'[75] Brent Scowcroft, President Bush Senior's National Security Adviser, concurred. In 1997, he said: 'We clearly would have preferred a coup. There's no question about that.'[76] The *New York Times* columnist Thomas Friedman, a guard dog of US foreign policy, was more to the point. What Washington wants is 'an iron-fisted Iraqi junta', which would be 'the best of all worlds'.[77] The clear conclusion is that they want another Saddam Hussein, rather like the one they had before 1991, who did as he was told.

'Perhaps the most repulsive thing about the whole policy,' wrote Eric Herring, 'is that US and British decision-makers have exploited popular humanitarian sentiment for the most cynical *realpolitik* reasons. They have no desire for the Shi'ite majority to take control or for the Kurds to gain independence. Their policy is to keep them strong enough to cause trouble for Saddam Hussein while ensuring that Saddam Hussein is strong enough to keep repressing them. This is a direct descendant of British imperial policy from the First World War onwards [and is about the control] of Iraqi oil . . . Divide and Rule was and is the policy.'[78]

In 1999, the United States faced a 'genuine dilemma' in Iraq, reported the *Wall Street Journal*. 'After eight years of enforcing a no fly zone in northern [and southern] Iraq, few military targets remain. "We're down to the last outhouse," one US official protested. "There are still some things left, but not many."'[79]

There are still children left. Around the time that statement was made, six children died when an American missile hit Al Jumohria, a community in Basra's poorest residential area. Sixty-three people were injured, a number of them badly burned. 'Collateral damage,' said the Pentagon. I walked down the street where the missile had struck in the early hours; it had followed the line of houses, destroying one after the other. They are rebuilt now, and several of the families have moved away. A man sat on a doorstep with his small son. He told me he had lost two daughters, aged eight and ten. 'They died sleeping,' he said. His opaque face bore his enduring shock and unimaginable grief. I asked him if he had photographs of them. No, nothing. I asked other parents. They shook their heads, as if the question was strange. Of course, poor people do not own cameras. Women waiting in the hospital queues had asked me to take pictures of them and their infants, because they had none.

In the Sheraton Hotel in Basra, vast, decaying and almost empty, there is a shop in the lobby that is still open. It is owned by Nabil Al-Jerani, who used to make a living processing tourists' film. There are no tourists now. 'I do a few weddings,' he said. 'When the missile hit Al Jumohria, I went down there the next morning with my camera.' He photographed the two sisters whose father I had met. They are in their nightdresses, one with a bow in her hair, their bodies engraved in the rubble of their homes, where they had been bombed in their beds. I included his images in my film *Paying the Price*; they haunt me.

I flew to Washington in the hope of seeing Secretary of State Madeleine Albright to ask her about her statement that 'we think the price is worth it'. She was not available, alas, and her spokesman, Assistant Secretary of State James Rubin, agreed to an interview. In his mid-thirties, self-assured and ideological, Rubin is the model of the post-cold war 'spin doctor', a professional propagandist who can also be refreshingly candid. When UN Secretary-General Boutros Boutros-Ghali was effectively sacked by Albright for not being sufficiently malleable, it was Rubin who told the media: 'Dr Boutros-Ghali was unable to understand the importance of co-operation with the world's first power.'[80]

The interview took place at the State Department in a room decked with flags and prints from the War of Independence. Rubin's assistant, Price Floyd, a worried man, fussed about the nature of my questions and the time Rubin could spare me. Tension built. When Rubin arrived, it was clear he preferred giving what he called 'presentations' to the press. Much of what he said had little basis in fact.

For example: 'We [the United States] allocate billions of dollars' worth of food and medicine for the Iraqi people.' In fact, the United States gives not a dollar: all humanitarian aid is paid by the Iraqi government from oil revenues authorised by the UN Security Council. He said that American policy was 'not sanctions *per se*, but to deny Saddam Hussein's regime the funds they would otherwise have to rebuild their mad military machine . . . the sanctions that we've imposed have made sure that Saddam Hussein has not had access to hundreds of billions of hard currency that he could use to build up that mad military machine . . . to build new chemical weapons capabilities, to build new biological weapons capabilities . . .'

I asked him, 'Don't you think it's ironic that for many years the

United States helped Saddam Hussein obtain these weapons of mass destruction to use against his neighbours?'

'No, I don't find that ironic. Iraq's regime is responsible, that's who's responsible. The United States didn't gas the Kurds . . .'

'The seed stock for Saddam Hussein's biological weapons was supplied by the American Type Culture Collection, a company that's just down the road from here, in Rockville, Maryland.'

'I'm sure they've been prosecuted for it.'

'No, they had Commerce Department approval.'

'To suggest we were sanctioning the sale of chemical weapons to Iraq is ridiculous.'

'It's true. The Senate hearing in 1994 heard that this particular company was given Commerce Department approval to sell biological agents to Saddam Hussein. All the documents are in the Library of Congress.'

'Are you suggesting that kind of thing was a goal of the United States?'

'It happened, and I'm only suggesting it's ironic that the US gave such support to this dictator, and now imposes an embargo that is causing such suffering not to him, but to the civilian population.'

'The suffering is not our fault . . . they have enormous quantities of food and medicine available. They store it in warehouses; they don't distribute it.'

'The senior United Nations Co-ordinator denied this. He said 88 per cent of all humanitarian supplies were delivered within a week of entering the country. A report by the head of the UN Office of Iraq in New York says that 76 per cent of medicines are distributed and the rest kept as a buffer stock, as directed by the World Health Organisation.'

'If you take a careful look at that report, there are examples where the Iraqi government has imported food and medicine, then not distributed them . . .'

'More than 73 million dollars in food production supplies for Iraq are currently blocked in New York by your government. If what you are saying is true, why did Kofi Annan, the Secretary-General of the United Nations, recently criticise the United States for holding up 700 million dollars' worth of humanitarian supplies?'

'You'll have to ask him.'

He went on to argue that a report by Unicef, the UN Children's Fund, proved that where the Iraqi government was in charge of distribution, in the south of the country, it was to blame for a higher child-mortality rate. I pointed out that the report had stated the opposite, that 'the difference in mortality rates between the north and south cannot be attributed to the way the relief effort has been implemented.'

He retorted, 'If you'd like to give a speech, we can switch chairs.'

'I don't think it becomes a senior State Department official to speak like that.'

'Let me hear your speech.'

'Why have you misrepresented the Unicef report?'

'Our analysis is based on a wide variety of sources, not simply the Unicef report . . .'

'The chief United Nations official in Iraq, Hans Von Sponeck, has appealed to the United States and Britain to let supplies through. He said, "Don't fight the battle against Saddam Hussein on the backs of the civilian population."'

'Mr Von Sponeck is commenting on subjects beyond his competence.'

'He is commenting on the humanitarian situation, and he is the senior United Nations humanitarian official on the ground in Iraq . . . Mr Rubin, by what logic can an entire nation be held hostage to the compliance of a brutal dictator, simply because they are unlucky enough to live under his brutal regime?'

'Look . . . in the real world, real choices have to be made, and it's our view that to allow Saddam Hussein unchecked access to hundreds of billions of dollars in oil revenue would be a grave and clear and present danger to the world. We have to weigh our profound sorrow at the tragic suffering of the people of Iraq against the national security challenge that Saddam Hussein would pose to the world if he weren't checked by the sanctions regime and the containment policy.'

I asked if the choice he described had been summed up by Madeleine Albright when she said that the 'price' of half a million dead children was 'worth it'.

'That quote has been seriously taken out of context . . .'

I handed him a transcript of the interview given by Albright. Her words were in context.

'Well, we don't accept the figure of half a million . . .'

'It's from the World Health Organisation.' (And backed by Unicef.)

'It's derived from a methodology we don't accept. We do accept that in choosing, in making policy, one has to choose usually between two bad choices, not between a good choice and a bad choice, and unfortunately the effect of sanctions has been more than we would have hoped.'

'Why is the US bombing civilians in Iraq?'

'Our aircraft are there to prevent Saddam Hussein from raining hell down on his own people. If he was not shooting at our aircraft, we would not need to take out the surface-to-air missile sites.'

'Your aircraft are taking out shepherds, their children and their sheep. It's in a UN report.'

'That report was based primarily on Iraqi sources. Iraqi propaganda will do anything to misrepresent what went on . . .'

'I went to Iraq to investigate and I found it to be true.'

'Well, I don't know the facts [and] I'm not a military expert. You'll have to address that to the Pentagon.'

'Have you been to Iraq?'

'No, I don't think I would be very welcome there!'

'Then how can you speak with such authority about what is going on there?'

'I've spoken to a lot of people . . . What you have to understand is that Saddam Hussein invaded another country. It's about Iraq's violation of the basic rule of the international system. They are paying the price for that.'

'*Who* is paying the price?'

'We're trying to minimise the price for the people of Iraq . . . what you have to understand is that there is a real world and an ideal world.'

'Is it too idealistic to ask who pays the price in Iraq? We are not talking about Saddam Hussein, but innocents. Was it too idealistic to ask who paid the price in the Holocaust, and East Timor and other atrocious happenings around the world?'

'Well, the idea of comparing what's going on in Iraq with the Holocaust, I find personally offensive.'

'It's also known as a holocaust.'

'Well . . . to compare the [effects of] sanctions with the Holocaust is an offence to the people who died in the Holocaust.'

'You don't think the deaths of half a million children qualify?'

'We've gone over that.'[81]

I flew on to New York for an interview with Kofi Annan, the Secretary-General of the United Nations. He appears an oddly diffident man, so softly spoken as to be almost inaudible.

'As the Secretary-General of the United Nations, which is imposing this blockade on Iraq,' I said, 'what do you say to the parents of the children who are dying?' His reply was that the Security Council was considering 'smart sanctions', which would 'target the leaders' rather than act as 'a blunt instrument that impacts on children'. I said the United Nations was set up to help people, not harm them, and he replied, 'Please do not judge us by what has happened in Iraq.'[82]

I walked across United Nations Plaza to the office of Peter van Walsum, the Netherlands' Ambassador to the UN and the chairman of the Sanctions Committee. What impressed me about this diplomat with life-and-death powers over 22 million people half a world away was that, like liberal politicians in the West, he seemed to hold two diametrically opposed thoughts in his mind simultaneously. On the one hand, he spoke of Iraq as if everybody was Saddam Hussein; on the other, he seemed to believe that most Iraqis were victims, held hostage to the intransigence of a dictator. He seemed a troubled man who, following the interview, sent me a gracious fax saying I could use the answers he had given to questions to which he had not agreed in advance.

I asked him why the civilian population should be punished for Saddam Hussein's crimes.

'It's a difficult problem,' he replied. 'You should realise that sanctions are one of the curative measures that the Security Council has at its disposal . . . and obviously they hurt. They are like a military measure.'

'Who do they hurt?'

'Well, this, of course, is the problem . . . but with military action, too, you have the eternal problem of collateral damage.'

'So an entire nation is collateral damage. Is that correct?'

'No, I am saying that sanctions have [similar] effects . . . I . . . you see . . . you understand, we have to study this further.'

'Do you believe that people have human rights no matter where they live and under what system?'

'Yes.'

'Doesn't that mean that the sanctions you are imposing are violating the human rights of millions of people?'

'It's also documented the Iraqi regime has committed very serious human rights breaches . . .'

'There is no doubt about that. But what's the difference in principle between human rights violations committed by the regime and those caused by your committee?'

'It's a very complex issue, Mr Pilger.'

'What do you say to those who describe sanctions that have caused so many deaths as "weapons of mass destruction", as lethal as chemical weapons?'

'I don't think that's a fair comparison.'

'Aren't the deaths of half a million children mass destruction?'

'I don't think that's a very fair question . . . We are talking about a situation which was caused by a government that overran its neighbour, and has weapons of mass destruction.'

'Then why aren't there sanctions on Israel [which] occupies much of Palestine and attacks Lebanon almost every day of the week? Why aren't there sanctions on Turkey, which has displaced three million Kurds and caused the deaths of 30,000 Kurds?'

'Well, there are many countries that do things that we are not happy with. We can't be everywhere. I repeat, it's complex.'

'How much power does the United States exercise over your committee?'

'We operate by consensus.'

'And what if the Americans object?'

'We don't operate.'[83]

In London, I sought an interview with Robin Cook, then the Foreign Secretary, another ambiguous figure, or so it seemed. A leading proponent of sanctions, he was also the inventor of the 'ethical dimension' in British foreign policy under New Labour (which has since been abandoned). My request was submitted in writing to the Foreign Office, and I was told there was 'a good prospect of a ministerial interview'. However, an official said that Cook was reluctant to be in a film 'next to images of dying babies', because this was 'an emotive issue', and he did not wish to be 'skewered'. I offered assurances that the interview would be straightforward and fairly edited, and said he could have most of the questions in advance.

After two months of to-ing and fro-ing, letters and phone calls and general stalling, Cook demanded an exclusive screening of the film, followed by an uncut ten-minute 'response' by him at the end. I replied that I wanted to conduct an interview with him, like everybody else in the film. His junior minister, Peter Hain, also wanted editorial control. I declined.

When *Paying the Price: Killing the Children of Iraq* went to air, triggering a significant public response, the Foreign Office produced a standard letter signed by Cook or Hain or an official. It exemplified the 'culture of lying' described by Mark Higson, the Iraq Desk Officer at the Foreign Office during the arms-to-Iraq scandals of the 1980s. Almost every word was misleading or false. These ranged from 'sanctions are not aimed at the Iraqi people' to 'food and medicines have never been covered by sanctions'. One of the most persistent lies was, 'Saddam Hussein has in warehouses $275 million worth of medicines and medical supplies, which he refuses to distribute.' The United Nations, right up to Kofi Annan, had refuted this. George Somerwill, the United Nations spokesman on Iraq, said, 'Not one of [the UN's] observation mechanisms has reported any major problem in humanitarian supplies being diverted, switched, or in any way misused.'

Then there was the $10 billion lie. 'Baghdad,' said Cook, 'can now sell over $10 billion of oil per annum to pay for food, medicine and other humanitarian goods.' Cook knew that more than a third went on reparations and UN expenses. This was topped by Peter Hain, who claimed that '$16 billion of humanitarian relief was available to the Iraqi people last year'. Citing UN documents, Hans Von Sponeck replied that the figure used by Hain actually covered four years and that, after reparations were taken out, Iraq was left with $100 for each human being it had to keep alive.

'Knowing what you know,' Von Sponeck accused Hain, 'you repeat again and again truly fabricated and self-serving misinformation.'

Hain: 'UN Resolution 1284 [continuing sanctions] represents the collective will of the Security Council.'

Von Sponeck: 'You know how deceptive this assertion is. Three out of five permanent members and Malaysia did not support this resolution.'[84]

Hain's enthusiasm for promoting sanctions has shocked those who remember him as a tenacious anti-apartheid campaigner and opponent of the American invasion of Indochina. Perhaps ambitious apostates are like that. He has even claimed 'there is no credible data' linking the use of depleted uranium by Britain and the US in Iraq with a sevenfold increase in cancers among the civilian population. As Professor Doug Rokke has shown, the evidence for the carcinogenic effects of depleted uranium is voluminous, from a warning in 1944 by Brigadier Leslie Groves, Director of the Manhattan Project, to numerous internal reports leaked from the Pentagon and Ministry of Defence. In 1991, the United Kingdom Atomic Energy Authority calculated that if 8 per cent of the DU fired in the Gulf War was inhaled, it could cause '500,000 potential deaths'.[85]

There is little doubt that if Saddam Hussein saw political advantage in starving and otherwise denying his people, he would do so. It is hardly surprising that he has looked after himself, his inner circle and, above all, his military and security apparatus. His palaces and spooks, like the cartoon portraits of himself, are everywhere. Unlike other tyrants, however, he not only survived, but before the Gulf War enjoyed a measure of popularity by buying off his people with the benefits from Iraq's oil revenue. Having sent his opponents into exile or murdered them, more than any Arab leader he used the riches of oil to modernise the civilian infrastructure, building first-rate hospitals, schools and universities.

In this way he fostered a relatively large, healthy, well-fed, well-educated middle class. Before sanctions, Iraqis consumed more than 3,000 calories each per day; 92 per cent of people had safe water and 93 per cent enjoyed free health care. Adult literacy was one of the highest in the world, at around 95 per cent.[86] According to *The Economist*'s Intelligence Unit, 'the Iraqi welfare state was, until recently, among the most comprehensive and generous in the Arab world.'[87]

It is said the only true beneficiary of sanctions is Saddam Hussein. He has used the embargo to centralise state power, and so reinforce his direct control over people's lives. With most Iraqis now dependent on the state food rationing system for their day-to-day survival, organised political dissent is all but unthinkable. In any case, for most Iraqis, it is cancelled by the sense of grievance and anger they feel towards the external enemy, western governments. In the relatively open and pro-western society that existed in Iraq before 1991, there was always the prospect of an uprising, as the Kurdish and Shi'a rebellions that year showed. In today's state of siege, there is none. That is the unsung achievement of the Anglo-American blockade.

Of this, ignorance is assured. 'Most Americans,' wrote Roger Normand, 'are unaware that sanctions against Iraq have killed more people than the two atomic bombs dropped on Japan, because the media have focused exclusively on the demonised figure of Saddam Hussein and presented Iraq as a country of military targets rather than people.'[88] By making the connection between the barbarism of western policy and that of the tyrant, opponents of sanctions are often called 'dupes'. (The late James Cameron, a journalist who was no stranger to this abuse, once told me, 'If they call you a dupe, you know you're getting something right.')

This has been Peter Hain's unconscionable tactic, smearing principled whistle-blowers like Denis Halliday and Hans Von Sponeck: an ironic echo of the apartheid regime in South Africa calling the younger Hain 'a dupe of communism'. Perhaps this is the familiar ritual of denial by those who, having retreated from their past, are the keenest participants.

The playwright Arthur Miller was more charitable. 'Few of us,' he wrote, 'can easily surrender our belief that society must somehow make sense. The thought that the State has lost its mind and is punishing so many innocent people is intolerable. And so the evidence has to be internally denied.'[89]

The economic blockade on Iraq must be lifted for no other reason than it is immoral, its consequences inhuman. When that happens, says Scott Ritter, 'the weapons inspectors must go back into Iraq and complete their mandate, which should be reconfigured. It was originally drawn up for quantitative disarmament, to account for every nut, screw, bolt, document that exists in Iraq. As long as Iraq didn't account for that, it was not in compliance and there was no progress. We should change that mandate to qualitative disarmament. Does Iraq have a chemical weapons programme today? No. Does Iraq have a long-range missile programme today? No. Nuclear? No. Biological? No. Is Iraq qualitatively disarmed? Yes. So we should get the inspectors in, certify that, then get on with monitoring Iraq to ensure they do not reconstitute any of this capability.'[90] Iraq has already accepted back inspectors of the International Atomic Energy Agency.

UN Security Resolution 687 says that Iraqi disarmament should be a step 'towards the goal of establishing in the Middle East a zone free from weapons of mass destruction . . .' In other words, if Iraq gives up, or has given up, its doomsday weapons, so should Israel. After September 11, 2001, making relentless demands on Iraq while turning a blind eye to Israel will no longer work. 'The longer the sanctions go on,' said Denis Halliday, 'we are likely to see the emergence of a generation who will regard Saddam Hussein as too moderate and too willing to listen to the West.'[91]

Neither can the old double standard of justice apply. At the time of writing, forty-three countries have ratified the establishment of an International Criminal Court; sixty are needed. The United States opposes the court, fearing Americans will be indicted. Certainly, if Saddam Hussein is to be prosecuted, so should Ariel Sharon; and so should their Faustian sponsors in the West, past and present.

In a letter to the *New Statesman*, Peter Hain described as 'gratuitous' my reference to the possibility that he, along with other western politicians, might find himself summoned before the International Criminal Court.[92] It is not gratuitous. A report for the UN Secretary-General, written by Professor Marc Bossuyt, a respected authority on international law, says that the 'sanctions regime against Iraq is unequivocally illegal under existing human rights law' and 'could raise questions under the Genocide Convention'. His subtext is that if the new court is to have authority, it cannot merely dispense the justice of the powerful.[93]

A growing body of legal opinion agrees that the court has a duty, as Eric Herring wrote, to investigate 'not only the regime, but also the UN bombing and sanctions which have violated the human rights of Iraqi civilians on a vast scale . . . It should also investigate those who assisted [Saddam Hussein's] programmes of now prohibited weapons, including western governments and companies.'[94]

In 2000, Hain blocked a parliamentary request to publish the full list of law-breaking British companies. A prosecutor might ask why, then ask who has killed the most innocent people in Iraq: Saddam Hussein, or British and American policy-makers? The answer may well put the murderous tyrant in second place.

On my last night in Iraq, I went to the Rabat Hall in the centre of Baghdad to watch the Iraqi National Orchestra rehearse. I had wanted to meet Mohammed Amin Ezzat, the conductor, whose personal tragedy epitomises the punishment of his people. Because the power supply is so intermittent, Iraqis have been forced to use cheap kerosene lamps for lighting, heating and cooking; and these frequently explode. This is what happened to Mohammed Amin Ezzat's wife, Jenan, who was engulfed in flames. 'It was devastating,' he said, 'because I saw my wife burn completely before my eyes. I threw myself on her in order to extinguish the flames, but it was no use. She died. I sometimes wish I had died with her.'[95]

He stood on his conductor's podium, his badly burned left arm unmoving, the fingers fused together. The orchestra was rehearsing Tchaikovsky's *Nutcracker Suite*, and there was a strange discord. Reeds were missing from clarinets and strings from violins. 'We can't get them from abroad,' he said. 'Someone has decreed they are not allowed.' The musical scores are ragged, like ancient parchment. The musicians cannot get paper. Only two members of the original orchestra are left; the rest have set out on the long, dangerous road to Jordan and beyond. 'You cannot blame them,' he said. 'The suffering in our country is too great. But why has it not been stopped?'

It was a question I put to Denis Halliday one evening in New York. We were standing in the General Assembly at the United Nations, where he had been Assistant Secretary-General. Now crossing the empty chamber, its design and décor almost lost in time since the 1950s, I asked him if the answer lay in James Rubin's remark about the 'real world and the ideal world'.

'*This* is where the real world is represented,' he said. 'This is where democracy applies: one state, one vote. By contrast, the Security Council has five permanent members which have veto

rights. There is no democracy there; it does not in any way represent the real world. Had the issue of sanctions on Iraq gone to the
General Assembly, it would have been overturned by a very large
majority. We have to change the United Nations, to reclaim what
is ours. The genocide in Iraq is the test of our will. All of us have
to break the silence: to make those responsible, in Washington
and London, aware that history will slaughter them.'

THE GREAT GAME

To me, I confess that [countries] are pieces on a chessboard upon which is being played out a great game for the domination of the world.

Lord Curzon, Viceroy of India, 1898

We have 50 per cent of the world's wealth but only 6.3 per cent of its population. In this situation, our real job in the coming period . . . is to maintain this position of disparity. To do so, we have to dispense with all sentimentality . . . we should cease thinking about human rights, the raising of living standards and democratisation.

George Kennan, US strategic planner, 1948

This is World War Three.

Thomas Friedman, New York Times, 2001

'War is never pleasant,' declared the liberal *Independent on Sunday* during the Gulf War in 1991. 'There are certain actions that a civilised society can never contemplate. This carpet

bombing is undeniably terrible. But that does not make it wrong.'[1]
In another war, in paddy fields not far from Saigon, I watched
three ladders curve in the sky, and as each rung reached the ground
there was a plume of fire and a sound that welled as thunder over
deep valleys, rippling and erupting rather than exploding. These
were the bombs of three B-52s flying in formation, unseen above
the clouds. Between them they dropped about seventy tons of
explosives in what was known as a 'long box' pattern, the military
term for carpet bombing. Everything inside a 'box' is presumed
destroyed.

When I reached a village within the 'box', the street had been
replaced by a crater; people a hundred yards from the point of
contact left not even their scorched shadows, which the dead
at Hiroshima had left. There were pieces of limbs and the intact
bodies of children thrown into the air by the blast; their skin had
folded back, like parchment. Strange anxieties crowded the mind:
I was worried I might step on somebody and disturb the dying.
But they were all dead; instead, I slipped on the shank of a water
buffalo.

It was experiences such as this that led me to question the nature
of power imposed from a distance, not just by those above the
clouds, but by impeccable, faraway figures who order the mass
killing of people, and by those who justify their crimes by repre-
senting the victims as terrorists, or merely as numbers, without
names, faces and histories, or as the inevitable casualties of a superior morality.

Thirty years later, the British Defence Secretary, Geoffrey
Hoon, told Parliament, 'The use of cluster bombs [in Afghanistan]
is entirely appropriate. Against certain targets they are the best and
most effective weapons we have.'[2]

I was standing on the veranda of a hospital overlooking Hongai, a coal-mining and fishing town on the shores of beautiful Ha Long Bay in the Gulf of Tonkin, northern Vietnam. Dr Luu Van Hoat estimated that 10 per cent of the town's children were now deaf. 'It was as if a great drum beat in our heads,' he said. For three days in June 1972, American fighter-bombers flew fifty-two sorties against Hongai, round the clock. This is believed to be a record. Hongai was bombed, on and off, for six years: one of the heaviest and most concentrated bombings ever inflicted.

The town's other distinction was that it was one of the first targets for what was known then as a 'pellet bomb', the prototype of the cluster bomb. This new weapon discharged hundreds of fragments, many of them shaped like darts. At the only school, which was flattened, I found a letter in the rubble. It was written by a young girl called Nguyen Thi An. 'The children wrote many letters to themselves in those days,' said a teacher.

My name is Nguyen Thi An. I am fifteen years old. This letter comes to you from Hongai where I was born at the foot of the Bai Tho mountain and the murmur of the sea-waves lapping against the shore. I had just done the seventh form in the Cao Thang School. It was a glorious day and my mother had just told me to lay the table. My father had come from his work. [He was a miner.] The next thing I heard the siren and I hurried to the shelter nearby. I could hear the engines of the plane, then the explosions. When the siren went again, I came out. My mother and father were lying there, my brother, Nguyen Si Quan, and my sister, Nguyen Thi Binh, were covered in blood. My sister had pieces of metal in her and so did her doll. She kept shouting, 'Where is mother and father?

Where's my doll?' My street, Ha Long Street, has fallen down now. This is the end of my letter.

The street where the Nguyen family lived was hit by the new bombs. According to Dr Luu, the darts entered Thi An's sister, Binh, and continued to move around in her body for several days, causing internal injuries from which she eventually died an agonising death. The darts were of a type of plastic difficult to detect under X-ray; the designers, I later read, had intended this.

The more common form of cluster bombs, known in the United States as Rockeyes, were tested in neighbouring Laos. They exploded into about 160 canisters, or bomblets, half of which lay on the ground until an animal or a person stepped on them, or picked them up, as children often did. They then exploded. Thirty years later, they continue to kill and maim an estimated 20,000 people a year in Laos, a tiny country never at war with America, which was bombed as a sideshow to the destruction of Vietnam and Cambodia. With their lethal longevity, cluster bombs are designed purely for terror, as an 'anti-personnel' weapon, to use the military term.

The day Geoffrey Hoon said that cluster bombs were 'the best and most effective weapons we have', they were dropped on Gardez, a dirt-poor town in Afghanistan that had long fallen to the anti-Taliban forces. The casualty figures are not known. Certainly, seven people in one family of refugees were killed and three were badly injured. They were refugees, sheltering in buildings belonging to a United Nations landmine-clearing agency, which was destroyed. This irony went unremarked in the press; cluster bombs are landmines. The crucial difference from those banned under international treaty is that they are dropped from aircraft. At the time of writing, an estimated 70,000 American cluster 'bomblets' lie unexploded in Afghanistan, already the most landmined country in the world.[3]

This is the nature of the 'war against terrorism'. The historical lineage is not in doubt. The same B-52s that destroyed much of Indochina bombed lines of civilians in Afghanistan, fleeing Kunduz. 'I saw twenty dead children on the streets,' said Zumeray, a refugee. 'Forty people were killed yesterday alone [of an estimated 150 civilians killed in three days]. Some of them were burned by the bombs, others were crushed by the walls and roofs of their houses when they collapsed from the blast.'[4]

The siege of Kunduz ended in a dirt fort called Qala-i-Jhangi, a name that should resonate in the 'civilised' memory; 'civilised' is a word used a great deal these days. American and British special forces called in American bombers in support of the forces of a Northern Alliance warlord, General Rashid Dostum, an Uzbek faction leader whose reputation for brutality includes chaining men to the tracks of tanks and who has since been appointed deputy defence minister in the new government. The men inside the fort were Taliban prisoners-of-war. They were cluster bombed. Those who survived had oil poured on them and were set alight, or were shot with their hands tied behind their backs. Hundreds of prisoners were killed in this way.

'Surely, the point about civilisation,' wrote a *Guardian* columnist, Isobel Hilton, 'is that it does not descend lightly into terror and barbarism? . . . The Afghans, we hear, have a bent for savagery and it would be absurd to expect a war in Afghanistan to be fought by Queensberry rules. But whose war is this? . . . Were [the Americans and British] fighting by Dostum's rules or by their own? Or do we no longer bother with the distinction?'[5]

Nothing has changed. Not the clusters, which were tested in Vietnam. Not the shock to the liberal conscience when forced to acknowledge the truth that mass murder, 'terror and barbarism' are standard practice on 'our' side: only the technology is different. Not the concealment of true objectives in moral illusions by the richest country on earth using its terrifying military might against the poorest, and in the name of 'civilisation'.

Neither has the disregard for peaceful resolution changed. In 1954, US Secretary of State John Foster Dulles walked out of a Geneva conference because the majority had agreed on democratic elections in Vietnam that would unify the north and south of the country. His action ignited a war that took five million lives.

Similarly, in the aftermath of September 11, 2001, the possibility of a peaceful resolution was sabotaged. The leaders of Pakistan's two Islamic parties said they had negotiated Osama bin Laden's extradition to Pakistan, even though the Americans had supplied no evidence with which to prosecute him for the Twin Towers attack. He was to be held under house arrest in Peshawar. The plan was approved by bin Laden himself and the Taliban leader, Mullah Omah. An international tribunal would then hear evidence and decide whether to try him or hand him over to America. A delegation of Islamic clerics from Pakistan, supporters of the Taliban, met Mullah Omah in Kandahar and told him that Pakistan would be plunged into crisis if Osama bin Laden was not handed over. 'Anyone who is responsible for this act, Osama or not, we will not side with him,' said the Taliban Information Minister. 'We told [the Pakistani delegation] to give us proof that he did it, because without that, how can we give him up?' Under pressure from Washington, Pakistan's President Musharraf vetoed the plan, which, said an American official, 'risked a premature collapse of the international effort' to capture bin Laden.

Perhaps we shall never know if the proposal was genuine or might have been successful. When the bombing of Afghanistan began, the US and British governments lied that 'no peaceful alternative was ever on offer'. Tony Blair said, 'There is no diplomacy with bin Laden or the Taliban regime . . . There is no compromise possible with such people . . . just a choice: defeat it or be defeated by it.' George W Bush said, 'I gave them a fair chance.'[6]

In the spirit of Lord Curzon's 'great game', the bombing of Afghanistan replaced unwanted tribes with preferred tribes. That both groups, in the vernacular of the modern game, are 'terrorists' is beside the point. The difference is that President Bush calls the present occupiers of Kabul, the Northern Alliance, 'our friends'. These are the same people welcomed with kite-flying in 1992, who then killed an estimated 50,000 in four years of internecine feuding. 'In 1994 alone,' reported New York-based Human Rights Watch, 'an estimated 25,000 people were killed in Kabul, most of them civilians, in rocket and artillery attacks. One-third of the city was reduced to rubble.'[7] Today, having tortured and executed hundreds of prisoners-of-war, as well as looted foreign aid warehouses, the new heroes have quietly re-established their monopoly over the heroin trade; this is not yet news.

There is no 'war on terrorism'. No such war is possible when the 'coalition' waging it consists of some of the leading terrorist states in the world – Algeria, Turkey, Russia, China, Indonesia – falling in with the United States. The search for Osama bin Laden is circus spectacle. The goal is the control, through vassals, of former Soviet Central Asia, a region rich in oil and minerals and of great strategic importance to competing powers, Russia and China. By February 2002, the United States had established permanent military bases in all the Central Asian republics, and in Afghanistan, whose post-Taliban government is American approved. 'America will have a continuing interest and presence in Central Asia of a kind that we could not have dreamed of before [September 11],' said Secretary of State Colin Powell.[8] This is just a beginning. The ultimate goal is a far wider American conquest, military and economic, that was planned during the Second World War and which, as Vice-President Cheney says, 'may not end in our lifetimes'.

Once the Taliban had retreated south from Kabul, Cheney and Defence Secretary Rumsfeld made this clear. America was planning action against 'forty to fifty countries'. Somalia, allegedly a 'haven' for the Islamic cult, al-Qa'ida, joins Iraq at the top of a list of potential targets. Rumsfeld disclosed that he had asked the Pentagon to 'think the unthinkable', after having rejected its 'post-Afghanistan options' as 'not radical enough'.[9] He did not mention that Somalia and part of the north-western Indian Ocean are a major oil and gas reserve, perhaps as large as the Caspian Sea. There, too, American companies have staked claims and await the imposition of a pro-western regime. There is no evidence that al-Qa'ida has bases in Somalia. The Americans are listening to a clan militia called Rahanwein, supported by and grinding the axe of neighbouring Ethiopia, which has long sought to keep Somalia weak and divided.

September 11 provided Bush's Washington with a remarkable justification. Pakistan's former Foreign Minister, Niaz Naik, was told by American officials in mid-July 2001 that military action against Afghanistan would go ahead by the middle of October.[10] Secretary of

State Colin Powell was then travelling in Central Asia, already gathering support for an anti-Afghanistan war 'coalition'. For Washington, the real problem with the Taliban was not their human rights violations; these were irrelevant. At first welcomed by Washington, the Taliban did not have total control of Afghanistan; *mujaheddin* factions held territory in the north. For this reason, to the Americans, the regime lacked 'stability', the control required of all clients.

It was this lack of 'stability' that deterred investors from continuing to finance oil and gas pipelines from the Caspian Sea, whose largely untapped fossil fuels of the Caspian Basin have become central, if not critical, to American planning. In 1998, Dick Cheney, then a consultant on pipelines to several Central Asian republics, told a conference of oil industry executives, 'I cannot think of a time when we have had a region emerge as suddenly to become as strategically significant as the Caspian.'[11]

Western interest in the Caspian goes back to the era when oil was being discovered, and exploited for the first time. Near the end of the nineteenth century, Russia fought to keep John B Rockefeller's Standard Oil Company out of the Caspian. The journalist John Reed, chronicler of the Russian Revolution, asked an audience at the 1919 People's Congress of the East, in Baku, the capital of Azerbaijan: 'Do you know how they pronounce Baku in the United States? Oil!'

Not only America and the European imperial powers wanted the Caspian oilfields. Hitler, in his invasion of Russia, and before running short of fuel and being defeated at Stalingrad, planned 'to take the saving prize of Caspian resources, and then to drive south for the even greater prize of Persia and Iraq', as a contemporary journalist, John Rees, has pointed out.[12]

For the West, the existence of the Soviet Union barred the way to oil and gas reserves, whose potential excited constant speculation. The largest inland sea was said, perhaps optimistically, to contain a third of the world's oil and gas reserves. The most extensive fields are in Kazakhstan and Azerbaijan, with smaller fields in Turkmenistan and Uzbekistan. Following the demise of the Soviet Union, the United States, Russia, China, France, Britain and Germany have competed in an 'oil rush' reminiscent of the imperial scramble for Africa.

In the 1990s, the United States staked its claim with several demonstrations of its 'global reach', such as the well-publicised deployment of 500 paratroopers from the 82nd Airborne Division in North Carolina to the desert of Kazakhstan. At the time, this was the longest airborne operation in military history and meant to demonstrate, said a Pentagon general, 'there is no nation on the face of the earth that we cannot get to', adding the apparent afterthought that the US was concerned with promoting 'independent, sovereign states that are able to defend themselves'.[13]

President Clinton's Energy Secretary, Bill Richardson, candidly described the former Soviet republics as 'all about America's energy security'. He said, 'We would like to see them reliant on western commercial and political investment in the Caspian, and it's very important to us that the pipeline map and the politics come out right.'[14]

The 'pipeline map' is critical, as the oil and gas are worthless without the means to carry them to deep-water ports. There are three routes a pipeline can go: through Russia, Iran or Afghanistan. For Washington, dependence on Russia is anathema, and Iran is the country America has spent more than twenty years isolating. It was not surprising that, in 1996, when the Taliban took power in

Kabul, they found themselves courted by the American oil lobby with its eye on 'one of the great prizes of the twenty-first century', as the *Daily Telegraph* reported. 'Oil industry insiders say the dream of securing a pipeline across Afghanistan is the main reason why Pakistan, a close political ally of America's, has been so supportive of the Taliban, and why America has quietly acquiesced in its conquest of Afghanistan.'[15]

Following September 11, 2001, none was more fervent in calling for the overthrow of the Taliban than the *Wall Street Journal*. However, five years earlier, the authentic voice of American capital had struck an entirely different tone. The Taliban, the paper declared, 'are the players most capable of achieving peace in Afghanistan at this moment in history'. Moreover, their success was crucial to secure Afghanistan as 'a prime trans-shipment route for the export of Central Asia's vast oil, gas and other natural resources'.[16]

Not only were the Taliban welcomed by Washington, Taliban leaders were flown to Texas, then governed by George W Bush, and entertained in Houston by senior executives of the oil company Unocal. According to George Monbiot, 'the company suggested paying these barbarians fifteen cents for every thousand cubic feet of gas it pumped through the land they had conquered.'[17] A Clinton administration official commented that Afghanistan would become 'like Saudi Arabia', an oil colony with no democracy and the legal persecution of women. 'We can live with that,' he said.[18]

In 1998, Unocal's Vice-President for International Relations, John J Maresca, told a Congressional inquiry that 'by 2010, western companies could increase oil production to 4.5 million barrels a day, an increase of more than 500 per cent in fifteen years'. He appealed for 'the development of appropriate investment climates in the region'. By this, he meant that 'construction of the pipeline we have proposed across Afghanistan could not begin until a recognised government is in place that has the confidence of governments, lenders and *our company* [emphasis added].' He made no mention of the barbaric nature of the regime, or of the al-Qa'ida terrorists it was said to entertain.

When Unocal eventually signed a 'memorandum of understanding' to build the pipeline from Turkmenistan to Pakistan via Afghanistan, it did so on behalf of a consortium of Enron, Amoco, British Petroleum, Chevron, Exxon and Mobil. The deal-makers were Dick Cheney, former Defence Secretary and future Vice-President, James Baker, former Secretary of State, and Brent Scowcroft, former National Security Adviser to the President. All had served in the Cabinet of George Bush Senior; Cheney and Baker are steeped in the oil industry; Cheney is perhaps the most powerful figure in the White House as I write; and Baker remains highly influential, as of course does Bush Senior, the 'oil man's president'.[19] A piquant postscript is that Bush Senior remains a paid consultant to the bin Laden family through the Carlyle Group and has met the family twice.[20]

The deal fell through when two American embassies in east Africa were bombed and al-Qa'ida was blamed. The *frisson* between Washington and the Taliban, however brief, has since moved on to the Caspian's oil republics, all of them sporting appalling human rights records. As the bombing of Afghanistan got under way, Rumsfeld promised 'tens of millions of dollars' to Tajikistan and Uzbekistan, which share 900 miles of border with Afghanistan.[21]

The Russians are not unhappy with this arrangement, believing the republics will move closer to Moscow as a counterweight to the Americans. Vladimir Putin's collaboration has won favours in Washington, such as the prospect of further strategic arms reductions and the licence to proceed with his own 'war on terrorism' in Chechnya, where an estimated 20,000 people have been killed. As American bombers were at work, Putin was being entertained by George W Bush at his Texas ranch. 'He is my new close friend,' said Putin, waving from a golf cart.

The other principal member of the 'coalition against terrorism', China, was the quickest off the mark with its condolences following September 11, 2001. From potential foe to friend in six months, China was rewarded with firm US support for its entry into the World Trade Organisation. Sanctions on the sale of military equipment, imposed following the Tiananmen Square massacre in 1989, have been eased so that the Chinese military can buy parts for American Black Hawk helicopters supplied in the 1980s. The issue of Tibet and multiple Chinese human rights abuses are now, like the human rights abuses of the Taliban in 1996, irrelevant.

Turkey, the only Muslim state in Nato, has been given IMF and World Bank loans on American instructions. The Turkish state's relentless ethnic cleansing of its Kurdish minority is another irrelevance. Pakistan's military dictatorship has been relieved of a western embargo imposed after the testing of nuclear weapons and its IMF and World Bank loans have been 'rescheduled'. The US Senate has rushed through a bill allowing Pakistan to receive emergency military aid. All of this follows an established pattern. The 'coalition' that attacked Iraq in 1991, led by the United States, was also put together with some of the biggest bribes in history.

A new 'world order' is evolving, yet the goals and even the vocabulary of Lord Curzon's day are retained. Following September 11, in his zeal to speak for the President of the United States, Tony Blair came closer to an announcement of real intentions than any British leader since Anthony Eden. Indeed, Blair bears a prime ministerial likeness not to Churchill, his acolytes' favourite, but to Eden, the last of Britannia's *ancien régime*, who attacked Egypt over Suez. In an evangelical speech to the Labour Party Conference soon after September 11, Blair served notice that imperialism's return journey to respectability was under way.

Having sent British forces off to war four times since he came to power in 1997 (Iraq, Yugoslavia, Sierra Leone, Afghanistan), Blair now invoked 'morality' to justify these and future actions. It is one of his favourite words; he once used it eleven times in a speech to a conference on press ownership organised by Rupert Murdoch. The bombing of Yugoslavia was a 'moral crusade'; Nato's mission is 'entirely moral', etcetera.

Now hark the Christian gentleman-bomber's vision of a better world for 'the starving, the wretched, the dispossessed, the ignorant, those living in want and squalor, from the deserts of northern Africa to the slums of Gaza to the mountain ranges of Afghanistan.' Hark his 'abiding' concern for the 'human rights of the suffering women of Afghanistan' as he colluded in bombing them and preventing food from reaching their starving children. (On September 16, the *New York Times* reported that Washington 'demanded . . . the elimination of truck convoys that provide much of the food and other supplies to Afghanistan's civilian population.' Blair subsequently rejected appeals by the international relief agencies for a pause in the bombing.)

As Frank Furedi reminds us in *The New Ideology of Imperialism*, it is not long ago 'that the moral claims of imperialism were seldom questioned in the west. Imperialism and the global expansion of the western powers were represented in unambiguously positive terms as a major contributor to human civilisation.' The quest went wrong when it was clear that fascism, with all its ideas of racial and cultural superiority, was imperialism, too, and the word vanished from academic discourse. In the best Stalinist tradition, imperialism no longer existed.[22]

Since the end of the cold war, a new opportunity has arisen. The economic and political crises in the developing world, largely the result of post-colonialism, such as the blood-letting in the Middle East and the destruction of commodity markets in Africa, now serve as retrospective justification for imperialism. Although the word remains unspeakable, the western intelligentsia, conservatives and liberals alike, boldly echo the preferred euphemism, 'civilisation'. From Italy's Prime Minister Silvio Berlusconi, an ally of crypto-fascists, to the former British liberal editor Harold Evans, the new imperialists share a concept whose true meaning relies on an unexpressed contrast with those who are 'uncivilised', i.e. inferior, and might challenge the 'values' of the West, specifically its God-given right to control and plunder.

There are many blueprints for the new imperialism, but none as cogent as that of Zbigniew Brzezinski, adviser to several presidents and one of the most influential gurus in Washington, whose 1997 book is said to have biblical authority among the Bush gang and its intelligentsia. In *The Grand Chessboard: American Primacy and its Geostrategic Imperatives*, Brzezinski writes, 'Ever since the continents started interacting politically, some 500 years ago, Eurasia has been the center of world power.'[23]

He defines Eurasia as all the territory east of Germany and Poland, stretching through Russia and China to the Pacific Ocean and including the Middle East and most of the Indian sub-continent. The key to controlling this vast area of the world is Central Asia. Dominance of Turkmenistan, Uzbekistan, Tajikistan and Kyrgyzstan ensures not only new sources of energy and mineral wealth, but a 'guardpost' over American control of the oil of the Persian Gulf.[24] 'What is most important to the history of the world?' wrote Brzezinski. 'The Taliban or the collapse of the Soviet empire? Some stirred-up Muslims or the liberation of central Europe . . . ?'[25] The 'stirred-up Muslims' replied on September 11, 2001.

The first priority has been achieved, says Brzezinski. This is the economic subjugation of the former superpower. Once the Soviet Union had collapsed, he writes, the United States looted some $300 billion in Russian assets, destabilising the currency and ensuring that a weakened Russia would have no choice but to look westward to Europe for economic and political revival, rather than south to Central Asia. Brzezinski's analysis dismisses the notion of 'local wars as responses to terrorism'. Rather, they are the beginning of a final conflict leading inexorably to the dissolution of national governments and world domination by the United States.

Nation states will be incorporated in the 'new order', controlled solely by economic interests as dictated by international banks, corporations and ruling elites concerned with the maintenance (by manipulation and war) of their power. 'To put it in a terminology that harkens back to the more brutal age of ancient empires,' he writes, 'the three grand imperatives of imperial geostrategy are to prevent collusion and maintain security

dependence among the vassals, to keep tributaries pliant and protected, and to keep the barbarians from coming together.'[26]

It may have been easy once to dismiss this as a message from the
far right. But Brzezinski is also the mainstream; he was President
Carter's National Security Adviser and has been influential with
Bush Senior, Clinton and now Bush Junior. His students include
Madeleine Albright and John Negroponte, the mastermind of
American terror in Central America, now Bush's Ambassador to
the United Nations. As US Ambassador to Honduras in the early
eighties, Negroponte oversaw the regime's funding of death squads
known as Battalion 3-16, which wiped out the democratic opposition. He administered the CIA's 'contra' war of terror against
neighbouring Nicaragua. A month after the Twin Towers attack,
Negroponte wrote to the UN Security Council that 'America's
self-defence . . . requires further actions with regard to other
states.' He was warning the world.[27]

'The hidden hand of the market,' wrote Thomas Friedman, the
guardian of American foreign policy in the *New York Times*, 'will
never work without a hidden fist. McDonald's cannot flourish
without McDonnell Douglas, the designer of the F-15. And the
hidden fist that keeps the world safe for Silicon Valley's technolo-
gies is called the US Army, Air Force, Navy and Marine Corps.'[28]

True American power is often described as economic: of one
country commanding more than a third of the world's resources,
with great companies like Microsoft and Motorola, Ford and
Coca-Cola more powerful than governments. This is a fashionable
view, not least in the anti-globalisation movement. 'Governments

are reduced to playing the role of servile lackeys to big business,' wrote Noreena Hertz, the dissident London financier. Even the US government had surrendered state power. She cited 'George W Bush's shameful obsequiousness to big energy corporations'.[29]

The illusion of a weakened state is the smokescreen thrown up by the designers of the 'new order'. Margaret Thatcher concentrated executive power while claiming the opposite; Tony Blair has done the same. The European project is all about extending the frontiers of the state. Totalitarian China has embraced the 'free' market while consolidating its vast state apparatus.

However, it is the American state that surpasses them all. It was triumphant and unscathed America that fashioned the present 'global economy' at a conference at Bretton Woods, New Hampshire, in 1944, giving America's military and corporate establishments unlimited access to minerals, oil, markets and cheap labour. The World Bank and the IMF were invented to implement this strategy. Their base is Washington, where they are joined by an umbilical cord to the US Treasury. Their members' voting power is determined by wealth: thereby America controls them. The president of the World Bank is always an American.

This is in line with George Kennan's historic dictum that America's 'real job' is to maintain its economic disparity with the rest of the world and 'cease thinking about human rights, the raising of living standards and democratisation'. Bretton Woods laid down the globalisation of poverty and the use of debt as a weapon. When John Maynard Keynes, the British representative at Bretton Woods, proposed a tax on creditor nations, designed to prevent poor countries falling into perpetual debt, he was told by the Americans that if he persisted, Britain would not get its desperately needed war loans. More than half a century later, the wealth gap between the richest 20 per cent of humanity and the poorest 20 per cent has doubled and an elite of fewer than a billion people controls 80 per cent of the world's riches. Through the agencies of Washington-run institutions, 'structural adjustment programmes' have secured an indebted imperium greater than the British Empire at its height.

'Globalisation does not mean the impotence of the state,' wrote the Russian economist and dissident Boris Kagarlitsky, 'but the rejection by the state of its social functions, in favour of repressive ones, irresponsibility on the part of governments and the ending of democratic freedoms.'[30] Since Thatcher and Reagan in the eighties, social democratic states have looked to America and progressively shed their 'social functions'. Repression has become a corollary. Following September 11, Congress enacted the so-called Patriot Act, which lays the foundation of a police state. More than two centuries of accrued constitutional 'checks and balances' have been diluted, some outlawed. Muslim-Americans have been arrested and imprisoned without trial; the Justice Department refuses to say how many. By executive order, George W Bush has set up secret military tribunals to try, imprison and execute foreign nationals in secret without recourse to any review or appeal system. Habeas corpus has been suspended for the first time since 1861. ('Anti-terrorist' legislation is also being enacted in Britain, as well as the large-scale abandonment of trial by jury. Similarly, in Australia, amended secrecy laws make government 'leaks' as serious a crime as espionage.)

'The atmosphere is such,' wrote Andrew Stephen, the *New Statesman*'s Washington correspondent, 'that supposedly liberal columnists debate the pros and cons of torturing prisoners, and then finally conclude that, yes, torture is OK in these extraordinary times.'[31] This evokes the McCarthy period of the fifties when a state-promoted paranoia consumed much of American life, suspending the Bill of Rights and dictating foreign policy. Obeying the totalitarian impulses that are as American as the Fourth of July, the United States has become a plutocracy.

The unelected Bush cabal consists of authentic fundamentalists, the heirs of John Foster Dulles and his brother Alan, the Baptist fanatics who ran the State Department and the CIA respectively, smashing reforming governments in country after country – Iran, Iraq, Guatemala – tearing up international agreements, such as the 1954 Geneva accords on Indochina. The difference is that, in the fifties, American capital was all-powerful. Potential rivals, Europe, Asia and the Soviet Union, were weak. Today, writes John Rees, '[America's] ability to underwrite the economic stability of the system [of global capitalism] has declined greatly in the post-war period. And the social and political instability that results from this fact constantly throws up challenges to US power.'[32]

The most unpredictable challenge is from the economic turmoil and divisions that globalisation has generated among the majority of humanity. In 1991, the plight of the least developed nations ('LDCs' or, in the new power jargon, 'failed states') was the subject of an ambitious programme of action launched by a United Nations LDC conference in Paris. Or so it appeared.

Ten years later, virtually every commitment made at Paris has been broken. The poorest countries are worse off than in 1990; the assertion that 'liberalisation' and 'trickle down economics' 'create wealth' is a mockery. The number of poor countries has actually increased, with almost half their people subsisting on less than a dollar a day. Their life expectancy has deteriorated to twenty-five years lower than that of people in developed countries; in Afghanistan, few survive beyond their forties.

The World Bank now admits that few of the poorest countries will meet its 'poverty reduction targets' by 2015. In other words, 'structural adjustment programmes', consisting of privatisation, indebtedness and the destruction of public services, have further impoverished and disaffected a large proportion of the world's population.[33]

In the poor and least developed world, people sense that a system of triage now determines whether they and their families live or die. Triage is the wartime division of wounded into those thought likely to survive, who are treated, and those left to die. When tariffs and food and fuel subsidies are eliminated under an IMF diktat, small farmers and the landless know they have been declared expendable. They join the 750 million people already under-employed, and unemployed.[34] The World Resources Institute says the toll of globalisation reaches 13–18 million child deaths every year; or 12 million children under the age of five, according to the UN Development Report.[35] 'If 100 million have been killed in the formal wars of the twentieth century,' wrote Michael McKinley, 'why are they to be privileged in comprehension over the annual [death] toll of children from structural adjustment programmes since 1982?'[36] He quoted Lester C Thurow's view that 'the tragedy afflicting humanity [was] neither metaphor, nor simile, of war, but war itself.'[37]

From this has come a popular resistance movement of unprecedented range: from the Landless People's Movement in Brazil to the anti-privatisation campaigns of Asia and Africa, to the great public demonstrations in the West, such as those in Seattle and

Genoa. Common to all these mass movements is the sense that ordinary people are under occupation, as in war. A friend, who was briefly prime minister of an 'LDC', one of the poorest countries, told me, 'I would watch the World Bank people fly in on a Monday and leave on the Wednesday. In their attaché cases was all they needed to know – the models of what our economy should be, regardless of the reality on the ground. They spent most of their time in the Intercontinental [hotel], having meetings with those who told them what they wanted to hear. It was the same with the IMF. The British government had soothing words about debt cancellation, but it all came down to buying British goods and contracting British firms. Profit was the word they never spoke, but it hung in the air. If we even hinted we'd repudiate any of this, we would be warned, sometimes crudely, that there was no other way; yet our only hope was to break out of it.'

This was illustrated at the fourth annual meeting of the World Trade Organisation at Doha, in the Gulf state of Qatar, in November 2001. Although the WTO has 143 members, only twenty-one governments, the richest, are permitted to draft policy, most of which has already been written by the 'quad': the United States, Europe, Canada and Japan. These rich nations demanded a new 'round' of what they call 'trade liberalisation', which is the power to intervene in the economies of poor countries, to demand privatisation and the destruction of public services. Only they are permitted to protect their home industries and agriculture; only they have the right to subsidise exports of meat, grain and sugar and to dump them in poor countries at artificially low prices, thereby destroying the livelihoods of small farmers. (In India, says the environmentalist Vandana Shiva, suicides among poor farmers are 'an epidemic'.)

Before the conference opened, the US trade representative Robert Zoellick invoked the 'war on terrorism'. He said, 'The United States is committed to global leadership of openness and understands that the staying power of our new coalition depends on economic growth . . .'[38] The implication could not be clearer. 'Economic growth' (rich elite, poor majority) equals anti-terrorism. Mark Curtis, the historian and Christian Aid's head of policy, who attended Doha, described 'an emerging pattern of threats and intimidation of poor countries' that amounted to 'economic gunboat diplomacy'. He said, 'It was utterly outrageous. Wealthy countries exploited their power to spin the agenda of big business. The issue of multinational corporations as a cause of poverty was not even on the agenda; it was like a conference on malaria that does not even discuss the mosquito.'[39] 'If I speak out too strongly,' said an African delegate, 'the US will phone my minister. They will say that I am embarrassing the United States. My government will not even ask, "What did he say?" They will just send me a ticket tomorrow . . . so I don't speak, for fear of upsetting the master.'[40] Haiti and the Dominican Republic were threatened with the withdrawal of their special trade preferences with the United States if they objected to the new 'round' of 'free trade'.

In Doha, the British government announced that it would give £20 million to help poor countries 'formulate trade policies and engage in the WTO'. Trade Minister Baroness Symons described the offer as a 'package of new measures'. The Blair Government has distinguished itself with statistical trickery, repeating announcements of the same 'new' money for domestic health and education spending. The 'new' £20 million for poor countries was first pledged in December 2000, then again in March 2001. In all three statements, Secretary of State Clare Short said she was 'doubling' British aid. This was false.[41] Her 'international development' portfolio comes from the same Orwellian lexicon as Blair's 'moral' bombing.

The truth about the West's various claims to furthering the 'development' of the poor world, 'forgiving' its debt and generally promoting 'poverty reduction' can be found in the statistics on foreign aid. Although members of the United Nations have agreed that the rich countries should give a minimum of 0.7 per cent of their Gross National Product in genuine aid to the poor world, Britain gives just 0.34 per cent and the United States barely registers, with 0.19.

Two illustrations tell the story. One of Clare Short's enterprises is in Ghana where, according to internal documents, British officials have made clear that aid money for a clean water project is conditional on the privatisation of the country's water supply. This would reap profits for at least one British multinational company, while ensuring the doubling of water bills for the poorest.[42] In the last Foreign Aid bill passed by the US Senate in 2000, a pittance of $75 million went to the poorest countries, a tenth of the cost of one B-52 bomber. The same bill approved $1.3 billion for the Colombian military, one of the world's worst human rights violators.

September 11 has strengthened Thomas Friedman's 'hidden hand' of globalisation, perhaps as never before. America's economic wars are now backed by the perpetual threat of military attack on any country, without legal pretence. Vivid confirmation of this is supplied by the US Space Command in a remarkable public document entitled *Vision for 2020*.

> Historically, military forces have evolved to protect national interests and investments — both military and economic. During the rise of commerce, nations built navies to protect and enhance their commercial interests. During the westward expansion of the continental United States, military outposts and the cavalry emerged to protect our wagon trains, settlements and railroads. The emergence of space power follows both of these models . . . Although unlikely to be challenged by a global peer competitor, the United States will continue to be challenged regionally. The globalisation of the world economy will continue, with a widening gap between 'haves' and 'have-nots' . . .

These challenges are to be met by 'Full Spectrum Dominance', allowing 'the medium of space, the fourth medium of warfare — along with land, sea and air — to close the ever-widening gap between diminishing resources and increasing military commitments.'[43]

The planners of 'Full Spectrum Dominance' realise that a great deal still has to be done on earth before the torch is passed to General Howell M Estes III, the Space Commander in Chief. Following the end of the cold war and the justification for American military dominance, the United States staged three 'demonstration wars'. The first came at the end of the valedictory year of 1989 when the Berlin Wall came down. The target was Panama, a small central American country known for its canal and poverty.

The United States invaded Panama with helicopter gunships and special forces, killing thousands of people in the poorest barrio of Panama City. The American reporter Martha Gellhorn, who went to investigate a year later, estimated 'at least 8,000 dead'.[44] These deaths, which received almost no media attention, were the price paid for the arrest of General Manuel Noriega, the Panamanian leader whose crime was running drugs (the United States was then testing its 'war on drugs' as a replacement for the cold war).

In circumstances less tragic, this would have been hilarious. Noriega was an old pal of George Bush Senior, who knew him when he was director of the CIA and Noriega was an Agency 'asset'. Drugs have long been a CIA currency. Like other client dictators, Noriega became uppity and stopped taking orders. His country was invaded and thousands were killed, so that he could be kidnapped. He is now serving life in a Florida prison. This terrible pantomime was no more than an excuse. The US was anxious to reimpose its sovereignty over the Panama Canal through a stooge more reliable than Noriega. The invasion was, perhaps above all, a demonstration of American resolve to others contemplating going their own way in the post-cold war years. As Henry Kissinger pointed out, 'Sometimes the US, in its wisdom, has to demonstrate its military prowess at crucial junctions of its history.'

The second demonstration war was the response to Iraq's invasion of Kuwait in 1990. The aim was to show US dominance of the oilfields of the Middle East (see above, 'Paying the Price'). It was followed, at the end of 1992, by the invasion of Somalia. Code-named 'Operation Restore Hope', this road-tested a strategy called 'humanitarian intervention', which was designed to replace the 'war on drugs'. When US Marines came ashore in Somalia 'to feed the starving', *Time* published a two-page colour photograph showing Somali children reaching out to a US Marine for 'the gift of hope'.[45] In fact, the famine was by then well over.

A convenient Noriega-type demon appeared in the person of General Mohammed Farah Aidid. A 'warlord' who had previously agreed to negotiate with the UN, Aidid became the principal bad guy whom the Marines set out to capture 'dead or alive'. Only then would the looting of food stocks end, said the Pentagon. It was all a familiar fable. Food stocks were being looted because there was not enough food. There was not enough food because Somalia had been left bankrupt by the murderous regime of Mohammed Siad Barre, an American client who had joined in the 'great game' of defeating Soviet influence in the Horn of Africa, having switched sides. There was also the question of Somalia's oilfields. Aidid was merely the leader of one of fifteen factions fighting to fill the vacuum and, like the Taliban and the Northern Alliance in Afghanistan, no more or less rapacious than his rivals. (The US is currently funding General Aidid's son, Hussein Aidid, who claims he can lead them to 'al-Qa'ida terrorists'.)

The invasion of Somalia served to distract attention from frantic attempts by President George Bush Senior, then in his political twilight following his defeat by Bill Clinton, to pardon those who might implicate him in the crimes of the Iran-Contra scandals. Operation Restore Hope resulted in the deaths of between 7,000 and 10,000 Somalis.[46] These figures, a CIA estimate, were not, to my knowledge, published in the mainstream media, which concentrated on the outrage of the deaths of eighteen Americans, later canonised in a Hollywood movie called *Black Hawk Down*, similar to the lying films that followed the Vietnam war, celebrating the invaders as victims.

In the aftermath of the bombing of Afghanistan, *The Guardian*'s diplomatic correspondent wrote that 'eighteen US soldiers were brutally killed [in Somalia] in 1993', offering 'an opportunity to settle an old score'.[47] Again, no mention was made of the thousands of Somalis who were brutally killed by the bringers of the 'gift of hope'.

Almost a decade after the 1991 Gulf War, the American photographer Ken Jarecke spoke about censorship by omission in the 'free' press. His was the breath-catching picture of an Iraqi burned to a blackened cinder, petrified at the wheel of his vehicle on the Basra Road where, along with hundreds of others, he was incinerated by American pilots during their 'turkey shoot' of retreating Iraqis and foreign nationals, mostly 'guest-workers', trapped in Kuwait.

The *Observer* alone published the picture, though not on the front page where it belonged. In the United States, it was suppressed until long after the war was over. This one image stripped away the propaganda that 'Desert Storm' had been an almost bloodless war: 'clean' and 'surgical'. 'No one would touch my photograph,' said Jarecke. 'The excuse was that it was too upsetting and people didn't want to look at that kind of thing any more. The truth was that the whole US press collaborated in keeping silent about the consequences of the Gulf War and who was responsible.'[48]

Jean Baudrillard's thesis that the Gulf War did not take place was dismissed at the time as the ramblings of an other-worldly French philosopher. However, as Phil Coles has pointed out, 'his basic claim that what we witnessed was purely a media performance aimed to assert US military authority over the globe was clear enough, and seems just as pertinent now.'[49]

As the media age is often confused with an information age, it is understandable that we have war by media. The 'open' and occasionally critical reporting of the Vietnam War was a lesson to western militarists. When George Bush Senior invaded Panama, no journalist witnessed the destruction of a swathe of Panama City. Only later was a 'pool' of reporters allowed limited access, and they were told that General Noriega's men, not helicopter gunships, had torched the slums. Press conferences became 'events': arenas for dispensing propaganda, such as entertaining videotapes showing 'surgical' bombing of alleged 'military facilities'. Here, military claims could be made without journalists being able to authenticate them.

What was striking during the Gulf War was how few journalists questioned the truth of these images, or enquired how the tapes were edited. They, like the commentators at home, were in thrall to the 'very accuracy of the new weapons', as the BBC's David Dimbleby excitedly put it.[50] In fact, less than 7 per cent of the weapons used in Desert Storm were 'smart', as the Pentagon admitted long after the war. Seventy per cent of the 88,500 bombs dropped on Iraq and Kuwait – the equivalent of seven Hiroshimas – missed their targets completely, and many fell in populated areas. The launch sites of Iraq's Scud missiles were said to have been 'knocked out'. Not one was destroyed.[51] None of this was reported at the time. Journalists were lied to and, accepting the lies, passed them on to the public.

The Basra Road, which Ken Jarecke photographed, was only one of many massacres. The others were not reported, having been carried out beyond the scrutiny of the 'press pool'. Unknown to journalists, in the last two days before the ceasefire, American armoured bulldozers were ruthlessly deployed, mostly at night, to bury Iraqis alive in their trenches, including the wounded. Six months later, *New York Newsday* disclosed that three brigades of the US First Mechanised Infantry Division 'used snow plows mounted on tanks and combat earth movers to bury thousands of Iraqi soldiers — some still alive — in more than 70 miles of trenches.' A brigade commander, Colonel Anthony Moreno, said, 'For all I know, we could have killed thousands.'[52]

The only images of this atrocity to be shown on television were used, bizarrely, as a backdrop to a discussion about the reporting of the war on a late-night BBC arts programme, with the participants apparently oblivious to the disturbing scenes on the screen behind them.[53] General Schwarzkopf's policy was that Iraqi dead were not to be counted.[54] 'This is the first war in modern times where every screwdriver, every nail is accounted for,' boasted one of his senior officers. As for human beings, 'I don't think anybody is going to come up with an accurate figure for the Iraqi dead.'[55] In fact, Schwarzkopf did provide figures to Congress, indicating that at least 100,000 Iraqi soldiers had been killed. He offered no estimate of civilian casualties.[56]

Shortly before Christmas 1991, the Medical Educational Trust in London published a comprehensive study of casualties. Up to a quarter of a million men, women and children were killed or died as a direct result of the American-led attack on Iraq.[57] This confirmed American and French intelligence estimates of 'in excess of 200,000 deaths'.[58] The sheer scale of this killing never entered public consciousness in the West.

The famous American TV anchorman Dan Rather told his national audience: 'There's one thing we can all agree on. It's the heroism of the 148 Americans who gave their lives so that freedom could live.' In fact, a quarter of them had been killed, like their British comrades, by other Americans. Moreover, official citations describing how Americans had died heroically were fake.[59]

When great truths are omitted, myths take their place, and the nature and pattern of great power are never explained to the public. Instead, militarism is presented as a morality play. Once again Blair applied his moral whitewash. 'Whatever faults we have,' he said, 'Britain is a very moral nation with a strong sense of right and wrong. That moral fibre will defeat the fanaticism of these terrorists and their supporters.'[60]

He was not referring to the fanatics who deliberately caused so many deaths in Iraq, Yugoslavia and Afghanistan. By any true moral light, the pretence that these crimes did not happen is itself a crime. The Orwellian twist is that the crime is justified by its 'ethical dimension'.

Although it has since been abandoned as an embarrassment, an 'ethical dimension' was the ambition ascribed to New Labour's foreign policy by the former Foreign Secretary Robin Cook. It was, for a while, a brilliant ruse. Instead of 'putting human rights at the centre of British foreign policy', as Cook promised, the British Government pursued, as normal, policies that ignored human rights or fostered their violation.

With an arms business second only in size to that of the United States, Britain continued to sell two-thirds of its lethal weapons and military equipment to governments with appalling human rights records. Its biggest customer is Saudi Arabia, the most extreme Islamic regime on earth, tutors of the Taliban and home to most of the alleged September 11 hijackers. An investigation by the National Audit Office into the £20 billion 'Al Yamamah' (The Dove) arms deal, whose report both Conservative and Labour governments refused to release, describes 'commissions' paid on Tornado fighters – £15 million on one aircraft is said to be the going rate.

Britain is a major arms supplier to at least five countries with internal conflict, where the combined death toll runs to almost a million people. Countries on the verge of war with each other are also clients: for example, India and Pakistan. For twenty years, Britain armed the Indonesian genocidists in East Timor.

When the Blair Government came to power, and Cook made his 'mission statement' at the Foreign Office, he met the two 1997 Nobel Peace Prize-winners, Bishop Carlos Belo and José Ramos-Horta, of East Timor. He assured them Britain would not license weapons that might be used for internal repression in their occupied country. At a public meeting in London soon afterwards, I listened to Bishop Belo make an emotional appeal to the government. 'Please, I beg you,' he said, 'do not sustain any longer a conflict which without these sales could never have been pursued in the first place, nor for so long.' He might have been speaking for much of humanity.

The government's response was to increase arms shipments to Indonesia under cover of the Official Secrets Act. These included Heckler and Koch machine guns used by General Suharto's special forces in East Timor, who had been identified as the source of the worst human rights abuses, including massacre and torture.[61] On September 11, 2001, as America was being attacked, the Blair Government was hosting an 'arms fair' in London's Docklands attended by various human rights abusers, including

Saudi Arabia, spiritual home of al-Qa'ida and birthplace of Osama bin Laden.

Out of respect for the victims of the Twin Towers atrocity, the annual conference of the Trades Union Congress was curtailed, along with sporting fixtures and other public events. The arms fair went ahead. Shortly afterwards, in an interview with David Frost, Blair declared that the way to defeat terrorists was to stop 'the people who gave them the weapons'. Frost said nothing.[62]

In the United States, the making and selling of arms is central to any economic 'boom'. The American 'military-industrial complex' is held aloft by arms and other military-related contracts. Forty cents in every tax dollar ends up with the Pentagon, which, in the financial year 2001/2, will spend more than $400 billion. War ensures the industry's prosperity. Following the Gulf War, American arms sales increased by 64 per cent. The Nato attack on Yugoslavia resulted in an extra $17 billion in sales. Following September 11, a 'boom' is already evident in the weapons business.

The day the stock markets re-opened after the attacks, the few companies showing increased value were the military contractors Raytheon, Alliant Tech Systems, Northrop Gruman and Lockheed Martin. As the US military's biggest supplier, Lockheed Martin's share value rose by 30 per cent. The company's main plant is in George W Bush's home state of Texas. As governor, Bush tried unsuccessfully to sell the Texas welfare system to Lockheed Martin-owned companies. In 1999, the company had record arms sales of more than $25 billion, and received more than $12 billion in Pentagon contracts.

Within six weeks of the Twin Towers attacks, Lockheed Martin had secured the biggest military order in history: a $200 billion contract to develop a fighter aircraft. The aircraft will be built in

Fort Worth, Texas, creating 32,000 new jobs. 'Amidst all the bad news these days,' said a company executive, 'what's happening to our stake in America is good news.'[63]

The British arms industry has also boomed since September 11. At the time of writing, BAE systems is selling a $40 million air defence system to Tanzania, one of the world's poorest countries. With a per capita income of $250 a year, half the population has no clean running water, and one in four children dies before their fifth birthday. Even though the World Bank has opposed the sale, Tony Blair has given it his personal backing, no doubt in the spirit of his evangelical speech to the Labour Party Conference in which he called Africa's poverty 'a scar on the conscience of the world'.[64]

With much of the Anglo-American media in the hands of the guardians of approved truths, the new imperialism, and the fate of faraway peoples, is reported and debated on the strict premise that the United States and British governments are opposed to violence as a means of resolving international disputes, and of course to terrorism. The issue invariably is how best 'we' can deal with the problem of 'them'.

The most salient truths remain taboos. In Britain, the first taboo is that British imperialism was not benign. Blair's pretensions in erecting a screen for present imperial actions also provide retrospective justification for the past. Generally, journalism and scholarship follow. For example, the reporting of apartheid in South Africa rarely mentioned the British role in laying the foundations of the apartheid system. In the 1950s, British behaviour in Malaya was little different from the American record in Vietnam, for which it proved inspirational: the withholding of food, villages turned into concentration camps and more than half a million people forcibly dispossessed.

American aircraft bombing the Middle East and Central Asia today refuel on the island of Diego Garcia in the Indian Ocean. Newsreaders often refer to it as 'uninhabited', but never say why. In 1966, in high secrecy and in defiance of the United Nations, the government of Harold Wilson expelled the entire population in order to hand the island over to the Americans in perpetuity as a nuclear arms dump and base. Until the islanders finally won a High Court action in 2000, almost nothing about their violent dispossession, and subsequent suffering in exile, appeared in the British media.

The second taboo is the longevity of the United States as both a terrorist state and a haven for terrorists. That the US is the only nation on record to have been condemned by the World Court for international terrorism (in Nicaragua), and has vetoed a UN Security Council resolution calling on governments to observe international law, is unmentionable. There is no conspiracy to keep this beyond public gaze. Compliance to institutional and corporate needs is internalised early in a journalist's career. The difference, in authoritarian societies, is that the state makes these demands directly. Self-censorship and censorship by omission are rarely pointed out to practising journalists and students in media colleges. Much of it is subliminal, giving it pervasive influence. Minimising the culpability of western power, indeed reporting countries in terms of their usefulness to the West, becomes almost an act of professional faith.

Passing moments are revealing. In a BBC broadcast in late 2001, Denis Halliday, the former Assistant Secretary-General of the

United Nations who resigned rather than administer what he described as a 'genocidal sanctions policy' in Iraq, incurred the indignation of the presenter, Michael Buerk. 'You can't possibly draw a moral equivalence between Saddam Hussein and George Bush [Senior], can you?' said Buerk. Halliday had referred to the needless slaughter by Bush's forces in the Gulf.[65] That the recent history of the West's true crimes makes Saddam Hussein 'an amateur', as Halliday put it, is another unmentionable.

Richard Falk, professor of international politics at Princeton, offers an explanation. Western foreign policy, he wrote, is propagated in the media 'through a self-righteous, one-way moral/legal screen [with] positive images of western values and innocence portrayed as threatened, validating a campaign of unrestricted violence.'[66]

In 1998, President Clinton went before the United Nations to speak on terrorism. 'What are our global obligations?' he asked. 'To give terrorists no support, no sanctuary.' Following September 11, 2001, President George W Bush said almost the same words. 'In the war against terrorism,' he said, 'we're going to hunt down these evil-doers wherever they are, no matter how long it takes.'[67] Strictly speaking, it should not take long, as more terrorists are given 'training, support and sanctuary' in the United States than anywhere on earth. They include mass murderers, torturers, former and future tyrants and assorted international criminals who fit the President's description. This is virtually unknown by the American public.

Hijacking is generally regarded as the gravest of crimes, especially since September 11. As William Blum points out in *Rogue State*, 'although there have been numerous air and boat hijackings over the years from Cuba to the US, at gunpoint, knifepoint and/or with the use of physical force, including at least one murder, it's difficult to find more than a single instance where the United States brought criminal charges against the hijackers.'[68] All the hijackers were anti-Castro.

As for sanctuaries, there is none to compare with Florida, currently governed by the President's brother, Jeb Bush. Blum describes a typical Florida trial of three terrorists, who hijacked a plane to Miami at knifepoint. 'This is like trying someone for gambling in a Nevada court,' he noted. 'Even though the kidnapped pilot was brought back from Cuba to testify against the men, the defence simply told the jurors the man was lying, and the jury deliberated for less than an hour before acquitting the defendants.'[69]

Former Guatemalan Defence Minister Hector Gramajo Morales was ordered by a US court to pay $47.5 million in damages for his responsibility for the torture of an American nun and the massacre of eight Guatemalans from one family. 'The evidence suggests,' said the judge, 'that Gramajo devised and directed the implementation of an indiscriminate campaign of terror against civilians.' Gramajo graduated from the Kennedy School of Government at Harvard, where he had studied on a US government scholarship. He was never arrested, and eventually returned home, saying he had merely carried out 'a more humanitarian' way of dealing with opponents of the regime.[70]

Former general José Guillermo García has lived in Florida since the 1990s. As head of El Salvador's military during the eighties, García oversaw the murder of thousands of people by death squads connected to the army. García's successor, General Carlos Vides Casanova, who ran the feared National Guard, is another resident of Jeb Bush's Sunshine State. 'According to the UN Truth

Commission for El Salvador,' writes Blum, 'Vides covered up and protected those who raped and murdered three American nuns and a lay worker in 1980. He was physically present on at least two occasions when Dr Juan Romagoza was tortured; in the end, the injuries inflicted on Arce left him unable to perform surgery.'[71]

General Prosper Avril, the Haitian dictator, liked to display the bloodied victims of his torture on television. When he was overthrown, he was flown to Florida by the US government. The notorious Haitian death squad leader Emanuel Constant, whose thugs terrorised Haiti, mutilating people with machetes, lives in New York. Armando Fernandez Larios, a member of a Chilean military squad responsible for torture and executions following the overthrow of Salvador Allende in 1973, lives in Miami. Argentine Admiral Jorge Enrico, who was associated with the infamous 'Dirty War' of torture and 'disappearances' in the 1970s, lives in Hawaii. Thiounn Prasith, Pol Pot's henchman and apologist at the United Nations, lives in Mount Vernon, New York.

In California, in the eighties, I met four Vietnamese who had been assassins in America's Operation Phoenix; one of them ran a fast food drive-in. He seemed a contented man. What all these people have in common, apart from their history of terrorism, is that they were either working directly for the US government or carrying out the dirty work of American policies. Operation Phoenix, for example, devised, funded and run by the CIA, was responsible for up to 50,000 murders.

Much was made of al-Qa'ida's training camps in Afghanistan, the target of American bombers. But these were kindergartens compared with the world's leading university of terrorism at Fort Benning in Georgia. Known until recently as the School of the Americas, it trained some 60,000 Latin American soldiers, policemen, paramilitaries and intelligence agents. Forty per cent of the Cabinet ministers who served in the genocidal regimes of Lucas García, Rios Montt and Mejia Victores in Guatemala are graduates.[72]

In 1993, the UN Truth Commission for El Salvador named the army officers who had committed the worst atrocities of the civil war; two-thirds of them had been trained at Fort Benning. They included Roberto D'Aubuisson, the leader of the death squads and the murderers of Archbishop Oscar Romero and a group of Jesuit priests. In Chile, the school's graduates ran Pinochet's secret police and three principal concentration camps. In 1996, the US government was forced to release copies of the school's training manuals. For aspiring terrorists, these recommended blackmail, torture, execution and the arrest of witnesses' relatives.

Renamed the Western Hemisphere Institute for Security Cooperation, or Whisc, the school's website is missing its 'History' pages. George Monbiot asked:

Given that the evidence linking the school to continuing atrocities in Latin America is rather stronger than the evidence linking al-Qa'ida training camps to the attack on New York, what should we do about the 'evil-doers' in Fort Benning, Georgia? Well, we could urge our governments to apply full diplomatic pressure and to seek extradition of the school's commanders for trial on charges of complicity in crimes against humanity. Alternatively, we could demand that our governments attack the United States, bombing its military installations, cities and airports in the hope of overthrowing its unelected government and replacing it with a new administration administered by the UN. In case this proposal proves unpopular with the American people, we could win their hearts and minds by dropping naan bread and dried curry in plastic bags stamped with the Afghan flag.[73]

Putting aside his mockery, Monbiot pointed out that the only moral difference between America's terrorism and that of al-Qa'ida is that the latter was puny by comparison.

The trail of blood is endless: from the subjugation of the Philippines and Central America, to the greatest terrorist acts of all, the bombing of Hiroshima and Nagasaki; from the devastation of Indochina, such as the murder of 600,000 peasants in neutral Cambodia, and the use of chemicals and starvation against civilian populations, to the shooting down of an Iranian passenger plane and the bombing of prisoners-of-war in a mud fort in Afghanistan.

The documentation of American terrorism is voluminous, and because such truths cannot be rationally rebutted, those who mention them, drawing the obvious connections between them, are often abused as 'anti-American', regardless of whether or not they themselves are American. During the 1930s, the term 'anti-German' was deployed against critics the Third Reich wished to silence.

'We need to get used to double standards,' said Robert Cooper, a foreign affairs adviser to Tony Blair in opposition.[74] In the media age, this is reinforced by the repetition of received truths disguised as news. For example, certain lives have media value while others are expendable. The killing of those of 'us' counts as a crime; the rest are unpeople.

When President Clinton ordered that missiles be fired at the Al-Shifa pharmaceutical plant in Sudan in 1998, claiming it was a 'chemical weapons facility', it was, by any measure, a major act of terrorism. The plant was well known as the only source of 90 per cent of the basic medicines of one of the poorest countries.

It was the only factory producing chloroquine, the most effective treatment for malaria, and anti-tuberculosis drugs that were lifelines to more than 100,000 patients at a cost of about £1 a month. Nowhere else produced veterinary drugs that killed the parasites passed from cattle to people, one of Sudan's main causes of infant mortality.[75]

As a result of the American attack, wrote Jonathan Belke of the Near East Foundation, a respected humanitarian organisation, 'tens of thousands of people – many of them children – have suffered and died from malaria, tuberculosis and other treatable diseases . . . [American] sanctions against Sudan make it impossible to import adequate amounts of medicines to cover the serious gap left by the plant's destruction.'[76]

How many Sudanese have since died as a result of Clinton's bombing? According to Germany's Ambassador to Sudan, 'several tens of thousands seems a reasonable guess.'[77] A United Nations investigation, requested by the Sudanese government, was blocked by Washington. None of this has been reported as news. When Noam Chomsky compared this terrorist act with the Twin Towers atrocity, he was abused by well-known commentators in the United States, including one who called him 'soft on fascism'.[78]

On no other subject are the boundaries of objective reporting more finely drawn than Israel. For thirty-five years at least, Palestinians have been denied a right of return to their homes, in breach of numerous United Nations resolutions and international law. In demanding Israel's withdrawal from the West Bank and Gaza, the Security Council used words strikingly similar to those that demanded Iraq's withdrawal from Kuwait in 1990. When Iraq did not comply, it was attacked by an American-led coalition and Kuwait was liberated. When Israel has not complied, it has received increased western, principally American, economic and military support.

With honourable exceptions, events in Palestine are reported in the West in terms of two warring rivals, not as the oppression of an illegal occupier and the resistance of the occupied. The Israeli regime continues to set the international news agenda. Israelis are 'murdered by terrorists', while Palestinians are 'left dead' after a 'clash with security forces'. Distinction is rarely made between a huge, nuclear-armed military force with tanks, fighter jets and helicopter gunships, and crowds of youths with slingshots. (The suicide bombers are a relatively recent phenomenon, the product mostly of the Israeli invasion of Lebanon, which left 17,500 dead.)

The BBC refers to Israel's policy of assassination as 'targeted killing', the euphemism used by Israeli spokesmen. It is rarely reported that of the hundreds killed and thousands wounded in the second *intifada*, 90 per cent have been Palestinian civilians, 45 per cent have been under eighteen, and 60 per cent were shot while in their homes, schools and workplaces.[79] Following the Gulf War, secret American-brokered deals in Oslo created the Palestinian Authority, leaving Palestinians corralled in apartheid-type bantustans on a fraction of their land. This is invariably reported positively and without explanation as 'the peace process'. (When he retired as the BBC's Middle East correspondent, Tim Llewellyn felt free to describe 'the peace process' as a 'misleading and humiliating farce'.)[80]

One of Tony Blair's successful media events was when he welcomed Yasser Arafat to Downing Street following September 11. Editorialists described Blair as a peacemaker, drawing a favourable comparison with the bellicose Bush administration. Indeed, the promotion of Blair as the steadying influence on Washington has been the main theme of Downing Street's 'spin' during the 'war on terrorism'. In fact, the meeting with Arafat was no more than a public relations exercise designed to placate the Arab world. It also served to disguise Blair's personal support for the Zionist project and his role as Ariel Sharon's closest ally in Europe. Little of this has been reported in the mainstream media.

Shortly after his election in 1997, Blair shamelessly appointed a friend, Michael Levy, a wealthy Jewish businessman who had fund-raised for New Labour, as his 'special envoy' to the Middle East, having first made him Lord Levy. This former board member of the Jewish Agency, who has both a business and a house in Israel and had a son working for the Israeli justice minister, was the man assigned to speak impartially to Palestinians and Israelis.

Under Blair, British support for Israeli repression has accelerated. During 2001, with 650 Palestinians killed by the Israelis, mostly civilians and many of them assassinations, the government approved ninety-one arms export licences to Israel, in categories that included ammunition, bombs, torpedoes, rockets, missiles, combat vessels, military electronic and imaging equipment and armoured vehicles. In answer to questions from George Galloway MP, Ben Bradshaw, the Foreign Office minister, said there was 'no evidence' that British arms and equipment had been used against Palestinians.[81] There is abundant evidence, such as Amnesty's report that the Apache helicopters used to attack the Palestinians are kept flying with British parts.[82]

The Blair Government has also supported the Israeli military-industrial complex by buying bullets, bombs, grenades and anti-tank missiles. The Metropolitan Police and South Wales Police buy Israeli ammunition. An Israeli combat aircraft training system was bought by the RAF. In 1999, a joint UK-Israeli high technology investment fund was established to underwrite joint research and development.

With no objections raised by the Blair Government, Israel hopes to open an army recruiting office in London – even though it would be recruiting for a war that stems from the occupation of Palestinian territories which the British government says is illegal. This will be a direct violation of the government's new anti-terrorism legislation; Israel's attacks on the Occupied Territories are, by any definition, terrorism, with their victims overwhelmingly civilians.

Blair's support for the Sharon regime goes even deeper. In May and July 2001, the authoritative *Jane's Foreign Report* disclosed that Britain and France had given 'the green light' to Sharon to attack Arafat if the Palestinian resistance did not stop. The British government was shown a plan for an all-out Israeli invasion and re-occupation of the West Bank and Gaza, 'using the latest F-16 and F-15 jets against all the main installations of the Palestinian Authority [and] 30,000 men or the equivalent of a full army'.

However, the Israeli plan needed a suicide bomb blast 'which causes numerous deaths and injuries. The "revenge" factor is crucial. It would motivate Israeli soldiers to demolish the Palestinians.'[83] What concerned Sharon and his inner circle, notably the author of the plan, Brigadier-General Shaul Mofaz, the Israeli Chief of Staff, was a secret agreement between Arafat and Hamas, the Islamic organisation responsible for most of the suicide attacks, that these attacks would be stopped in Israel proper. Following September 11, the Sharon regime worried that a Middle East 'solution' would be a bi-product of America's 'war on terrorism', especially when George W Bush blurted out a *non sequitur* that he had always backed the 'dream' of a Palestinian state. Something had to be done.

On November 23, 2001, Israeli agents assassinated the Hamas leader, Mahmud Abu Hunud. Twelve days later, the inevitable response came in co-ordinated suicide attacks against Israel. 'Whoever decided upon the liquidation of Abu Hunud knew in advance that that would be the price,' wrote Alex Fishman, the well-connected intelligence writer, in the Israeli daily *Yediot Achronot*. 'Whoever gave a green light to this act knew full well that he is thereby shattering in one blow the gentleman's agreement between Hamas and the Palestinian Authority [which was] not to play into Israel's hands by mass attacks on its population centres.'[84]

On cue, Sharon's forces attacked the Occupied Territories with unprecedented force, all but destroying the Palestinian Authority and Arafat's political base. The Americans issued the usual anodyne statement about 'ending violence', this time placing most of the responsibility on Arafat. There was no more loose talk of the 'dream' of a Palestinian state. Arafat, said Sharon, was now 'irrelevant'. Blair, the peacemaker, said nothing, along with almost all the western media.

Robert Cooper's call for double standards was answered eloquently in Kosovo. Unlike the Palestinians, the ethnic Albanian population of Kosovo was given an almost immediate right of return by the United States and its Nato partners. The western media overwhelmingly supported the Nato action. Yet this was a civil war, and Nato did not dispute Yugoslav sovereignty. While the Kosovars were being repatriated, 250,000 Serbs and Roma were expelled or fled in fear from the province. Nato's 40,000 occupying troops stood by as this ethnic cleansing took place and did virtually nothing to prevent the Kosovo Liberation Army from murdering, torturing, abducting, desecrating churches and generally living up to its previous description by Secretary of State Albright and Foreign Secretary Cook as 'a terrorist organisation'.

During the Kosovo 'war', the list of civilian targets in Yugoslavia was published on the internet, but no newspaper carried it. Codenamed 'Stage Three', these targets included public transport, non-military factories, telephone exchanges, food processing plants, fertiliser depots, hospitals, schools, museums, churches, heritage-listed monasteries and farms.

'They ran out of military targets in the first couple of weeks,' said James Bissell, the Canadian Ambassador to Yugoslavia. 'It was common knowledge that Nato then went to Stage Three: civilian targets. Otherwise, they would not have been bombing bridges on Sunday afternoons and market places.'[85] Admiral Elmar Schmahling, head of German Military Intelligence, said, 'The plan was to first put pressure on the civilian population and second to destroy the Yugoslav economy so deeply it would not recover.'[86]

During the latter weeks of the bombing, I watched the BBC's Kirsty Wark interviewing General Wesley Clark, the Nato commander, on *Newsnight*. She asked not one question about the targeting of civilians, even though the city of Nis had been recently sprayed with cluster bombs, killing women, old people and children caught in the open. That only 2 per cent of Nato's precision-guided missiles hit military targets was fleeting news. The headlines spoke of 'mistakes' and 'blunders'; barely a handful of journalists, notably Robert Fisk, exposed them as deliberate. The overall 'coverage' was exemplified by the work of Mark Laity, the BBC's correspondent in Brussels, soon afterwards appointed Personal Adviser to the Secretary-General of Nato.

The 'coverage' became a series of official justifications, or lies, beginning with US Defence Secretary William Cohen's claim that 'we've now seen about 100,000 military-aged [Albanian] men missing . . . they may have been murdered'. Two weeks later, David Scheffer, the US Ambassador at Large for war crimes, announced that as many as '225,000 ethnic Albanian men aged between 14 and 59' may have been killed. The British press took their cue. 'Flight from genocide', said the *Daily Mail*. 'Echoes of the Holocaust', chorused the *Sun* and *The Mirror*. Tony Blair also invoked the Holocaust and 'the spirit of the Second World War', apparently unaware of the irony. The Serbs, in their epic resistance to the Nazi invasion, lost more people, proportionally, than any other European nation.

By June 1999, with the bombardment over, international forensic teams began subjecting Kosovo to minute examination. The American FBI arrived to investigate what was called 'the largest crime scene in the FBI's forensic history'. Several weeks later, having not found a single mass grave, the FBI went home. The Spanish forensic team also returned home, its leader complaining angrily that he and his colleagues had become part of 'a semantic pirouette by the war propaganda machines, because we did not find one – not one – mass grave.'

In November 1999, the *Wall Street Journal* published the results of its own investigation, dismissing 'the mass grave obsession'. Instead of 'the huge killing fields some investigators were led to expect . . . the pattern is of scattered killings [mostly] in areas where the separatist Kosovo Liberation Army had been active.' The paper concluded that Nato stepped up its claims about Serb killing fields when it 'saw a fatigued press corps drifting toward the contrarian story: civilians killed by Nato's bombs.' Many of the claims of numbers killed could be traced back to the KLA. 'The war in Kosovo was cruel, bitter, savage,' said the *Journal*. 'Genocide it wasn't.'

Nato had bombed, according to British Defence Secretary George Robertson, 'to prevent a humanitarian catastrophe' of mass expulsion and killing. In December 1999, the Organisation for Security and Co-operation in Europe, whose monitors were in Kosovo just before the bombing, released its report, which went virtually unreported. It disclosed that most of the crimes against the Albanian population had taken place after the bombing began: that is, they were not a cause, but a consequence of the bombing. 'While Serb forces were clearly the instrument of the unfolding "humanitarian disaster",' wrote former senior Nato planner Michael McGwire, 'Nato's long-trailered urge to war was undoubtedly a primary cause [and description of the] bombing as "humanitarian intervention" [is] really grotesque.'

In the summer of 2000, the International War Crimes Tribunal, a body effectively set up by Nato, announced that the final count of bodies found in Kosovo's 'mass graves' was 2,788. This included Serbs, Roma and combatants. It meant that the figures used by the British and US governments and most of the media were inventions. Little of this was reported.

Those journalists who had swallowed Nato's lies were the loudest in their abuse of the few who had questioned the bombing and exposed the charade of the 'breakdown' of the Rambouillet talks that were manipulated to justify the bombing. The tactic of their abuse was to equate objections to the killing of civilians with support for Milosevic. This was the same propaganda that equated humane concern for the Iraqi and Afghan peoples with support for Saddam Hussein and the Taliban respectively. It is a time-honoured intellectual dishonesty. In the wake of September 11, 2001, the proponents of the 'war on terrorism' fortified themselves with the cry, 'We were right over Kosovo, we are right now' as the cluster bombs rained down again, with only a change of terrain.[87]

If Iraq is attacked in the 'war on terrorism', journalists will have played a leading, if routine, role. In the United States, the major newspapers and influential columnists, such as William Safire, have called for the 'next liberation'. Dissent is confined to an occasional reader's letter. Writing in the *Washington Post*, the columnist Michael Kelly spoke for the consensus in the media when he wrote, 'The American pacifists . . . are on the side of future mass murders of Americans. They are objectively pro-terrorist . . . that is the pacifists' position, and it is evil.'[88] In Britain, where some dissent has been allowed, the promotion of a justification for bombing is not as verbose, but constant.

'US HAWKS ACCUSE IRAQ OVER ANTHRAX', said the *Observer*'s front page on October 14, 2001. This 'conduit propaganda' was supplied by American intelligence. The anthrax used in the attacks in America was weapons-grade and, reported the *New York Times*, 'is virtually indistinguishable in critical technical respects from the anthrax produced by the US military'. The FBI described it as an 'inside job'.[89] In a subsequent article over two pages, headlined 'The Iraqi Connnection', the *Observer* quoted its unnamed 'intelligence sources' to link Iraq with September 11. 'The evidence is mounting . . .' it said, without facts, adding the rider that 'nothing gets close to identifying those ultimately responsible'.[90]

This is a form of journalism that hints, beckons, erects a straw man or two, then draws back. In a follow-up piece, the reporter, David Rose, concluded his barren inquiry with the proposal that, because Iraq was 'an ideal place to establish a bridgehead' to democracy in the Arab world, it should be attacked. 'There are occasions in history,' he wrote, 'when the use of force is both right and sensible. This is one of them.' His remarkable proposal was illustrated by a photograph of the Iraqi dictator with his famous fiendish grin. It is the cartoon face of an entire society. No mention was made of the fate of twenty-two million people, stricken from a decade-long blockade and held hostage to power politics over which they had no control, who now awaited their 'sensible' onslaught.

A not dissimilar article in *The Guardian,* by David Leigh and Jamie Wilson, was more subtle. Headlined 'Counting Iraq's Victims', their 'analysis' began by associating famous propaganda tales about 'dead babies' from the First World War and the Gulf War with contemporary United Nations studies that conclude that half a million Iraqi children have died, mostly as a result of the blockade. Astonishingly, they wrote that the 'dead babies of Iraq' never existed and were 'a statistical construct . . . the claims of America's critics'. They then contradicted this by acknowledging the UN and other authoritative sources. Their objection, it seemed, was that Osama bin Laden had used the conclusions of these studies to further his own propaganda, the logic being that a truth, however documented, was tainted when someone you did not like used it. Quixotically, they added, 'Bin Laden . . . does perhaps have a point.' To the casual reader, seeds of doubt had been sown. If Iraq's dead and dying babies were merely a 'statistical construct', why not bomb?[91]

The most important 'evidence' of Iraq's complicity with September 11 is that the alleged leader of the Twin Towers suicide hijackers, Mohamed Atta, was supposed to have met an Iraqi intelligence agent in the Czech Republic. In the British press, the intelligence agent was promoted from being 'low level' *(The Guardian)* to 'mid-ranking' *(Independent)* to 'senior' *(Financial Times)* to the 'head of Baghdad's intelligence services' *(The Times)*. Only the *Financial Times* questioned whether the 'meeting' took place at all, or had anything to do with the destruction of the Twin Towers.[92] On the BBC's *Newsnight*, Mark Urban, the Foreign Office correspondent, revealed that there was 'secret information' about 'a missile Saddam Hussein was planning to launch'. He provided no evidence.

The speciousness of the 'Iraq connection' was, in contrast, never headline news. Only the *Daily Telegraph* reported, on December 18, 2001, that Czech police denied that Mohamed Atta had ever visited the Czech Republic. Silence also prevailed when the *New York Times* of February 5, 2002, disclosed, 'The Central Intelligence Agency has no evidence that Iraq has engaged in terrorist operations against the United States in nearly a decade, and the agency is also convinced that President Saddam Hussein has not provided chemical or biological weapons to al-Qa'ida.'

Omission is the most virulent form of censorship. In much of the reporting of Afghanistan, the American assault on one of the world's poorest countries was justified with potent images evoking the Taliban's 'evil'. The persecution of women provided deeply offensive pictures of women shrouded in tent-like burqas, denied the most basic human rights. Although occasional reference was made to the Anglo-American role in the creation of the fanatical *jihadi* groups which spawned the Taliban, there was no mention of an extraordinary period in the recent past of this benighted society, an understanding of which would have cast 'our war for human rights and civilised values' (Blair) in its true perspective.

In the sixties, a liberation movement arose in Afghanistan, centred on the People's Democratic Party of Afghanistan (PDPA), which opposed the autocratic rule of King Zahir Shar and eventually overthrew the regime of the king's cousin, Mohammad Daud, in 1978. It was, by all accounts, an immensely popular revolution. Most foreign journalists in Kabul, reported the *New York Times*, found that 'nearly every Afghan they interviewed said [they were] delighted with the coup'.[93] The *Wall Street Journal* reported that '150,000 persons . . . marched to honour the new flag . . . the participants appeared genuinely enthusiastic.'[94] The *Washington Post* said that 'Afghan loyalty to the government can scarcely be questioned'.[95]

The new government outlined a reform programme that included the abolition of feudal power in the countryside, freedom of religion, equal rights for women and the granting of hitherto denied rights to the various ethnic minorities. More than 13,000 prisoners were freed and police files publicly burned.

Under tribalism and feudalism, life expectancy was thirty-five and almost one in three children died in infancy. Ninety per cent of the population was illiterate. The new government introduced free medical care in the poorest areas. Peonage was abolished; a mass literacy campaign was begun. For women, the gains were unheard of; by the late 1980s, half the university students were women, and women made up 40 per cent of Afghanistan's doctors, 70 per cent of its teachers and 30 per cent of its civil servants.

Indeed, so radical were the changes that they remain vivid in the memories of those who benefited. Saira Noorani, a female surgeon who escaped the Taliban in September 2001, said, 'Every girl could go to high school and university. We could go where we wanted and wear what we liked . . . We used to go to cafés and the cinema to see the latest Indian films on a Friday and listen to the latest Hindi music . . . It all started to go wrong when the *mujaheddin* started winning . . . They used to kill teachers and burn schools . . . We were terrified. It was funny and sad to think these were people the west had supported.'[96]

The problem with the PDPA government was that it was supported by the Soviet Union. Although Stalinist in its central committee structure, it was never the 'puppet' derided in the West, nor was its coup 'Soviet-backed', as western propaganda claimed at the time. In his memoirs, Cyrus Vance, President Carter's Secretary of State, admitted, 'We have no evidence of any Soviet complicity in the coup.'[97] On the other wing of the Carter administration was Zbigniew Brzezinski, Carter's National Security Adviser, who believed that the recent American humiliation in Vietnam required atonement, and that the gains of post-colonial liberation movements elsewhere presented a challenge to the United States. Moreover, the Anglo-American client regimes in the Middle East and the Gulf, notably Iran under the Shah, had to be 'protected'. Were Afghanistan to succeed under the PDPA, it would offer the 'threat of a promising example'.

On July 3, 1979, unknown to the American public and Congress, President Carter authorised a $500 million covert action programme in support of the tribal groups known as the *mujaheddin*. The aim was the overthrow of Afghanistan's first secular, progressive government. Contrary to cold war mythology, the Soviet invasion of Afghanistan, which did not happen until six months later, had nothing to do with it. Indeed, all the evidence is that the Soviets made their fatal move into Afghanistan in response to the very tribal and religious 'terrorism' that the Americans used to justify their invasion in November 2001.

In an interview in 1998, Brzezinski admitted that Washington had lied about the American role. 'According to the official version of history,' he said, 'CIA aid to the *mujaheddin* began during 1980, that is, after the Soviet army invaded Afghanistan . . . But the reality, secretly guarded until now, is completely otherwise.'[98] In August 1979, the US embassy in Kabul reported that 'the United States' larger interests . . . would be served by the demise of [PDPA government], despite whatever setbacks this might mean for future social and economic reforms in Afghanistan.'[99]

Thus, Washington began a Faustian affair with some of the most brutal fanatics on earth. Men like Gulbuddin Hekmatyar received tens of millions of CIA dollars. Hekmatyar's speciality was trafficking in opium and throwing acid in the faces of women who refused to wear the veil. Invited to London in 1986, he was lauded by Prime Minister Thatcher as a 'freedom fighter'. Between 1978 and 1992, the life of the PDPA government, Washington poured some $4 million into the *mujaheddin* factions. Brzezinski's plan was to promote an international movement that would spread Islamic fundamentalism in Central Asia and 'destabilise' the Soviet Union, creating, as he wrote in his autobiography, a 'few stirred-up Muslims'.

His grand plan coincided with the ambitions of the Pakistani dictator, General Zia ul-Haq, to dominate the region. In 1986, CIA director William Casey gave the CIA's backing to a plan put forward by Pakistan's intelligence agency, the ISI, to recruit people from around the world to join the Afghan *jihad*. More than 100,000 Islamic militants were trained in Pakistan between 1982 and 1992. (Taliban means 'student'.) Operatives, who would eventually join the Taliban and Osama bin Laden's al-Qa'ida, were recruited at an Islamic college in Brooklyn, New York, and given paramilitary training at a CIA camp in Virginia. This was called 'Operation Cyclone'.

In Pakistan, *mujaheddin* training camps were run by the CIA and Britain's MI6, with the British SAS training future al-Qa'ida and Taliban fighters in bomb-making and other black arts. This continued long after the Soviet army had withdrawn in 1989. When the PDPA government finally fell in 1992, the West's favourite warlord, Gulbuddin Hekmatyar, rained American-supplied missiles on Kabul, killing 2,000 people, until the other factions agreed to make him Prime Minister.

The last PDPA president, Mohammad Najibullah, who had gone before the UN General Assembly to appeal desperately for help, took refuge in the UN compound in Kabul, where he remained until the Taliban took power in 1996. They hanged him from a street light.[100]

A few months before September 11, I attended a conference at the University of Sussex on the 'new imperialism'. What was extraordinary was that it took place at all. Julian Saurin, who teaches at the School of Asian and African Studies, said that, in ten years, he had never known an open discussion on imperialism. About 80 per cent of international relations studies in the great British universities is concerned with the United States and Europe. Most of the rest of humanity is rated according to its degree of importance to 'western interests'.

The idea of a modern version of imperialism is provocative to the 'liberal realists' who shunned the Sussex conference and dominate international relations. They believe in it passionately, but have convinced themselves it is something else; some still call it *realpolitik*. The few who speak out are an embarrassment, or they are not true 'realists'.

The historian Niall Ferguson, a politics professor at Oxford, often utters the unmentionable. Applauding Blair's speech to the 2001 Labour Party Conference, with its language of moral gunboats and Gladstonian conviction of superior beings, Ferguson said, 'Imperialism may be a dirty word, but when Tony Blair is essentially calling for the imposition of western values – democracy and so on – it is really the language of liberal imperialism. Political globalisation is just a fancy word for . . . imposing your views and practices on others.' Only America could lead this new imperial world, he said.[101]

The study of post-war international politics, 'liberal realism', was invented in the United States, largely with the sponsorship of those who designed and have policed modern American economic power. They included the Ford, Carnegie and Rockefeller Foundations, the OSS (the forerunner of the CIA) and the Council on Foreign Relations, effectively a branch of government. Thus, in the great American universities, learned voices justified the cold war and its great risks.

In Britain, this 'transatlantic' view found its clearest echo. With honourable exceptions, scholars have taken the humanity out of the study of nations and congealed it with a jargon that serves the dominant power. Laying out whole societies for autopsy, they identify 'failed states' and 'rogue states', requiring 'humanitarian intervention'. As Chomsky points out, imperial Japan described its invasion of Manchuria as a 'humanitarian intervention' and Mussolini used the term to justify seizing Ethiopia, as did Hitler when the Nazis drove into Sudetenland.[102]

Today, there are minor variations. Michael Ignatieff, professor of human rights at Harvard and an enthusiastic backer of the West's invasions and bombing (as a way to 'feed the starving and enforce peace in case of civil strife'), prefers 'liberal intervention'.[103]

'Good international citizen', 'good governance' and 'third way' are from the same lexicon of modern imperial euphemisms adopted by the new 'progressive' movement in world affairs. In academic literature and the media, Bill Clinton was described as 'centre left', a denial of the historical record. During the Clinton years, the principal welfare safety nets were taken away and poverty in America increased, an aggressive missile 'defence' system known as 'Star Wars 2' was instigated, the biggest war and arms budget in history was approved, biological weapons verification was rejected, along with a comprehensive nuclear test ban treaty, the establishment of an international criminal court, a worldwide ban on landmines and proposals to curb money laundering. Contrary to myth, which blames his succes- sor, the Clinton administration effectively destroyed the movement to combat global warming. In addition, Haiti was invaded; the blockade of Cuba was reinforced; Iraq, Yugoslavia and Sudan were attacked.

'It's a nice and convenient myth that liberals are the peace- makers and conservatives the war-mongers,' wrote Hywel Williams, 'but the imperialism of the liberal may be more danger- ous because of its open-ended nature – its conviction that it represents a superior form of life.'[104]

Before he became a war leader, Tony Blair was fond of promot- ing the 'end of ideology' when, in fact, the ideology he shares with an entire political and media class is one of the most power- ful of the modern era. It is all the more pervasive for its concealed and often unconscious attachment to a status quo of inequity based on class and wealth.

While rejecting the labels of ideology, labelling others is popular. The most interesting label stuck on me says that I belong to the 'neo-idealist "left"'. The inverted commas around 'left' are not explained, nor is 'neo-idealist'. Timothy Dunne, of the International Politics Department at the University of Wales, Aberystwyth, labelled me in this way in a text book which distinguished itself by skating over the horrors perpetrated by General Suharto in East Timor.[105] This 'liberal realism' was not untypical among international relations academics, especially those extolling a 'third way', the jargon that obfuscates a reactionary agenda. For almost a quarter of a century, East Timor was a victim of their silence.

An invasion and occupation that wiped out a third of the population, causing more deaths, proportionally, than in Cambodia under Pol Pot, provoked an academic silence, broken only by John Taylor's *Indonesia's Forgotten War* (Zed Books) and the work of Peter Carey, Mark Curtis and, more recently, Eric Herring. The greatest genocide in the second half of the twentieth century apparently did not warrant a single substantial academic case study, based on primary sources, in a British university, liberal or traditional.

Those in charge of humanities teaching whisper complaints that universities have become vocational training colleges, obsessed with sponsorship. By keeping silent, they have allowed governments to diminish a wealth of knowledge of how the world works, declaring it 'irrelevant' and withholding funding. This is not surprising when the humanities departments – the engine rooms of ideas and criticism – are close to moribund. When academics suppress the voice of their knowledge, who can the public turn to?

There is no conspiracy, and that should be emphasised. It is simply the way the system works, ensuring 'access' and 'credibility' in an academic hierarchy always eager to credit more ethical intent to government policy-makers than the policy-makers themselves. In politics departments, the task of liberal realists is to ensure that western imperialism is interpreted as crisis management, rather than the cause of the crisis and its escalation. By never recognising western state terrorism, their complicity is assured. To state this simple truth is deemed unscholarly; better to say nothing.

Following September 11, the central issue again is silence. Who dares question the newly minted credo that the Twin Towers attackers were merely 'apocalyptic nihilists', who hated 'modernity' and 'civilisation'? Above all, who will say the 'war on terrorism' is fraudulent: that its prosecutors are themselves terrorists from a greater league and that their actions will, at the very least, produce more carnage and martyrs?

Among people of liberal heart, confusion about imperialist intentions as the United States attacks former clients and allies who have slipped the leash, declaring them new Hitlers, is perhaps understandable; but 'this mixture of bafflement in the face of the obvious and cryptic gesturing in the direction of truth', as David Edwards wrote, is now a luxury true civilisation can ill afford. The dangers are too urgent.[106]

'We are likely to see', Denis Halliday told me, 'the emergence of those who may well regard Saddam Hussein as too moderate and far too willing to listen to the West. That has already happened to the Palestinians. Such is the desperation of people whose children are dying in their thousands every month and who are bombed almost every day by American and British planes.'

Who else, like Halliday, will say that the function of the United

Nations is being reduced to the management of colonies? Who will put aside the chessboard and explain that only when great grievance, injustice and insecurity are lifted from nations will terrorism recede?

'The time has come when silence is betrayal,' said Martin Luther King. 'That time is now.'

THE CHOSEN ONES

There is something special about being an Australian. That Australian spirit, that capacity for mateship that allows us to pull together in times of challenge and times of adversity is something special.

Prime Minister John Howard

If there was a race between democratic nations to see who could best address the violation of the human rights [of its original people], Australia would be coming stone motherless last.

Professor Colin Tatz, Genocide Studies Centre, Sydney

Physically, there is no place like Sydney: the deep-water harbour, the tiara of Pacific beaches, the estuaries and secret bays where white eucalyptus, the giant ghost gums, rise from the water's edge. At the centre is a stage set like a small New York, its props the great arched bridge, the other-worldly Opera House and an Olympic pool, built in the 1930s with art-deco dolphins and an honour roll of 86 world swimming records, itself a world record. Beside the pool is Luna Park, a fun fair announced by a huge face with a slightly demented smile. This is Australia's façade, or 'showcase', as the promoters of the Olympic Games preferred. The 2000 Olympics were to herald 'a new golden age' with Australians, sang the jingle choir, 'the chosen ones to take the dream to the new millennium: a dream we all share'.

The chosen ones left nothing to chance. When the International Olympic Committee came to inspect the city before the prize was won, traffic lights were timed to turn green as their limousines approached. The fascist past of the IOC's president, Juan Samaranch, rated barely a mention in the Sydney press, and the radio in his hotel room was said to have been 'tuned' to avoid picking up a certain commentator who might raise the forbidden subject. Harbour cruises, lobster dinners, champagne, cognac and Cuban cigars came from what was known as a 'sucking-up fund' of $A28 million. Grants, each worth $A52,500, were handed out to African IOC delegates the night before the IOC voted. The President of the Australian Olympic Committee, John Coates, arranged a 'catering scholarship' for the daughter of the IOC representative of Swaziland. 'I am the father of six children,' said Coates. 'Isn't this what the Olympic family is all about?'[1]

On one junket to Sydney, the wife of an IOC delegate spotted a black man playing a didgeridoo at Circular Quay, where he is a tourist fixture.

'Who's that?' she enquired.

'An Aborigine,' replied one of her hosts.

'Really? Where are the rest of them?'

'Er, in the outback.'[2]

Sydney has a large Aboriginal ghetto at Redfern, a five-minute limo drive away. It is easily distinguished from the rest of the city by an oppressive police presence. The Aboriginal Legal Service, which is based in Redfern, tried to interest the IOC in visiting an Australia they had not seen, the one behind the postcard, but there was little time and the atmosphere was not conducive. 'Anyone who threatens Sydney's bid had better watch out!' declared the New South Wales Government minister responsible for the Olympics.[3]

At Monaco, where the IOC met to decide the winning bid, Australia was presented as an oasis of human harmony, in marked contrast to China, its main rival for the games. Delegates were treated to performances by Aboriginal dancers and didgeridoo-players in full body paint, together with cavorting giant kangaroos and wombats. White Australia has long appropriated the art and artefacts of the Aboriginal Dreaming, and not surprisingly the boomerang was adopted as the motif of the games. Two Qantas aircraft were repainted with indigenous designs. There was an 'indigenous advisory committee', headed by the affable former rugby star Gary Ella, himself an Aborigine, and a group of Aboriginal elders were designated 'official greeters'.

On September 15, 2000, when Cathy Freeman, a world-class runner and an Aborigine, carried the torch that lit the Olympic flame, all those embarrassing revelations of bribery and kickbacks were subsumed in the glow of a 'culturally correct' opening ceremony devoted to 'mutual respect and reconciliation'. Its motif was an Aboriginal dancer leading a white child on a mythical journey through Australian history while she was dreaming. (This came as a relief to those who remembered their nation's contribution to the closing ceremony at the Atlanta Olympics: inflatable kangaroos riding bicycles.)

The Kimberley region is in the remote north of Western Australia. It is a mysterious place of ancient, volcanic ground that can seem on fire in the dawn light, with escarpments like petrified waves and flora not found elsewhere in Australia or the world. The great boab tree, with its gnarled, twisted limbs, lives for up to 2,000 years. The massif known as Bungle Bungle, thrown up by a meteorite crater millions of years old, is a surreal, three-dimensional spectacle. People have been here for 40,000 years: the oldest human presence on earth.

Kununurra was built in 1960, in the heart of the Ord River irrigation farmland. The town reminded me of its equivalent in the South African *veldt*: manicured gardens, air-conditioned supermarkets with Toyota four-wheel drives outside, squinting, overweight, grey-skinned people, clubs and sporting facilities that are still all-white. Half the population, however, is black. Their paintings hang in the local hotel and on the wall of a bank. Their artefacts, copied in China, are on sale. But where are they? The only Aborigine I saw taking part in the life of the town was a man holding the Stop and Go sign at some roadworks. The rest are in the shadows: face down in the park, silhouettes framed in doorways, like figures on a gallows.

The Olympic torch came through here on its way to Sydney. Almost everyone was out to cheer it on, except those black people who could not see it, having been blinded by trachoma, a disease as old as the Bible. Australia is the only developed country on a World

Health Organisation 'shame list' of countries where children are still blinded by trachoma. Impoverished Sri Lanka has beaten the disease, but not rich Australia.[4]

Once hunter-gatherers in their traditional society, Aborigines had exceptional vision; now watch the old people stumble, many of them wearing cheap dark glasses and wiping streaming eyes. According to the Director of the Centre for Eye Research in Sydney, Professor Hugh Taylor, up to 80 per cent of Aboriginal children have potentially blinding trachoma because of untreated cataracts. 'This is inexcusable,' he said.[5]

I accompanied an Aboriginal Medical Services team making a spot check of children in and around Kununurra. A third were found to have trachoma. At Doon Doon school, half the fifty-six children were diagnosed with the disease. 'What if these were white children?' I asked Dr Alice Tippetts. She replied with a hand over her mouth; like Australian apartheid, it is the unspeakable. The disease is entirely preventable. An infection of the eyelids, it is spread in conditions of poverty, such as overcrowding and lack of clean running water and sewerage.

On the wall of the office of Dr Kim Hames, Western Australia's Minister for Aboriginal Affairs and Water Resources, is a didgeridoo and a Certificate of Appreciation from the Keep Australia Beautiful Council, 'for supporting Tidy Western Australia in May'. The death rate of Aborigines in the state is higher than that in Bangladesh. The son of a stockman, Dr Hames told me he had many Aboriginal friends, and believed the problem of trachoma would be 'washed away if only Aboriginal children had swimming pools'. His government was planning to build twelve swimming pools. When? He did not know. Why this plan had not been executed, along with the provision of proper housing with clean running water and sanitation, and surfaced roads in remote areas that keep down the dust, was lost in a convoluted explanation of a kind you often hear from Australian politicians; he seemed to be trying to share the blame between the victims themselves, for 'cultural habits that are millions of years old', and 'the Aboriginal bureaucracy'.

I asked, 'Is there another reason why these basics, like sealed roads, decent housing and recreational facilities, all the things that are standard in white Australia, are missing in Aboriginal areas?'

'Well, it's because [white] people feel that if you give a swimming pool to an Aboriginal community it is a luxury, and they are fine the way they are, living in the desert, like they've always done . . .'6

Dr Richard Murray, of the Kimberley Aboriginal Medical Services Council, whose patients are all Aboriginal, has studied the causes of their suffering. 'By most measures of indigenous health,' he told me, 'Australia is last in the world. The Aboriginal people suffer from diseases we saw the end of in the Edinburgh slums in the last century, like rheumatic fever. Here, it is the highest ever reported in the world. And diabetes, which affects up to a quarter of the adult Aboriginal population, causing kidney failure and diabetic blindness. And gastro-enteritis . . .'

'What's the cause?'

'Poverty and dispossession. Look at housing. Ninety per cent of overcrowded households in Australia are Aboriginal, and that's from two per cent of the population. What it comes fundamentally down to is a lack of political will to allocate resources. The Federal government spends about 25 per cent less per capita on the health of Aboriginal people compared to the rest of the population. Look at the phenomenon of suicide, which comes from a lack of opportunity and hope for the future. It is the young men who bear the brunt. In a typical community where there are, say, fifty men up to the age of twenty-five, one or two will kill themselves, two or three will try and another dozen will give it some serious thought. They come from families who have to live with constant grief, with not wanting to go to bed at night for fear of waking up in the morning to find someone hanging. It is a heart-wrenching truth that the world knows little about.'[7]

At Woorabinda, in Queensland, I drove in the dust behind Paul Gribble, who had the coffin of a two-month-old Aboriginal baby girl in the boot of his car. She was to be buried that afternoon following a funeral at Paul's church, St Matthew's. His father and grandfather were missionaries, and the line stops with him. Proud and disillusioned, and angry, he referred to 'an Aboriginal population incarcerated all these years in a prison built by us'.

Opening his register of deaths, he said, 'The first funeral I conducted, I was irritated by the people wailing, and I screamed out for them to shut up. And they did, and all the funerals thereafter were dead quiet. Then one day I stood up and apologised to them. I told them I was wrong, just as it is wrong that people continue to die as they do. Look at this list: babies, young men. And it's wrong the authorities harass them as they do. I am the chaplain at Rockhampton Prison, where a third of the prisoners are Aboriginal – from two per cent of the population.'[8]

Woorabinda came into existence in 1927 as one of five 'controlled' reserves that were part of an Australian gulag where people were dumped, bereft of community and family ties that matter to them sometimes more than life itself. The reserve was run by a 'chief protector', who exercised total power over those who were sent there: he could exile and punish people, pry into their sexual lives, confiscate their belongings, conceal their savings and commit the most recalcitrant to mental asylums. The legacy of that history, says Elizabeth Young, an Aboriginal health worker, is that 'the [Woorabinda] community now has no sense of itself and is slowly suiciding. Why? A lot of our schoolkids have dreams, but as they grow older and they start rebelling, they realise, they know, they've got no future, so they do exactly what their parents did before them; they begin to waste away. We have such clever and brilliant kids, for whom there is no help in taking that first step: a girl who might dance in Sydney, a stockman who might ride internationally, a footballer who might play for his country. Some get through, of course, mostly in sport, and their names are well known; but they are a tiny few. It seems most of the kids I grew up with and went to school with have died, and they shouldn't have died. They got on the grog and they wasted. In the last couple of weeks, here in Woorabinda, we've had a thirteen-year-old and a fifteen-year-old attempt suicide. No one's surprised.'[9]

In Woorabinda's cemetery, beyond Sebastopol Creek, the ants have bored holes in the white wooden crosses. There are children lying in row upon row: then young men in the next, and the next. Forty seems old here. I sat, incredulous. I am always left incredulous – there is no other word – whenever I come to this Australia, a country unknown to most of my white compatriots. If I were a black Australian, I would be dead by now. The life expectancy of Aborigines is up to twenty-five years shorter than whites, lower than in most countries and matched only in India and Central Africa.[10] Apart from countries at war, Australia has the distinction of having the highest death rate in the world – among its first people.[11]

In recent years, the health of Aboriginal women has so deteriorated that their death rate is six times that of white women. 'A certain kind of statistical deafness has developed,' wrote the Aboriginal and Torres Strait Islander Social Justice Commissioner. 'The meaning of these figures is not heard – or felt. The statistics of infant and perinatal mortality are our babies and children who die in our arms . . . The statistics of shortened life expectancy are our mothers and fathers, uncles, aunties and elders who live diminished lives and die before their gifts of knowledge and experience are passed on. We die silently under these statistics.'[12]

In white Australia, an enduring myth is the 'missing millions' of dollars that the Federal and state governments 'pour' into 'Aboriginal welfare'. It is the stuff of political and bar-room received wisdom, the fuel of bigotry, and it is false. Dr Murray in Kimberley had been referring to a nationwide health review, which disclosed, in 1997, that Aboriginal health care received 25 per cent less government funding per head of population than health care for whites. For every dollar spent per head under the national Pharmaceutical Benefits Scheme, only twenty cents were spent, per head, on Aboriginal people.[13]

I asked him why the myth had such stamina. 'It's part of the Australian psyche at some level,' he said. 'By believing that money has been spent and wasted, people move to the conclusion that conforms with what is in the backs of their minds: that the real reason is innate or genetic. More important, it allows white Australians to say it isn't their fault, it's the fault of Aboriginal people. A whole language of denigration backs this up – "they don't look after their kids, and if only they would wash themselves" – and allows the majority population to distance itself from the truth that our first nation continues to be denied essential citizenship rights: basic services, housing, a decent access to education, a hope for the future. That's why we're last in the world, particularly when compared with New Zealand, Canada and the US, which have comparable indigenous populations and where there has been significant progress in the last generation. In those countries, a baby born to indigenous people has a life expectancy of only three to six years less than the rest of the population. Here, the difference is eighteen to twenty years. The question is: what makes us different?'

When I interviewed Philip Ruddock, the Federal minister responsible for 'reconciliation' in time for the Olympic Games, he boasted that the Aboriginal child mortality rate had improved in recent years. He was right; it is now only three times that of white children. I reminded him that a fellow Federal Cabinet member, Dr Michael Wooldridge, the health minister, had made an extraordinary admission. 'In my area of health,' he said, 'there is no evidence of any improvement whatsoever in the last decade . . . the gap [between Aboriginal and white health] has actually widened.'[14]

Ruddock agreed that 'the Aboriginal statistics are truly appalling'. I said, 'I understand you have been a member of Amnesty International for twenty years.'

'That is correct.'

'How do you feel receiving Amnesty reports on human rights violations with "Australia" written across the top, such as: "Aborigines are still dying in prison and police custody at levels that may amount to cruel, inhuman and degrading treatment"?'

Smiling, he replied, 'Why do they use the word "may"?'[15]

Such a supercilious response is not uncommon in political Australia. During our interview, Ruddock made no attempt to challenge the facts of Aboriginal suffering, yet offered nothing that suggested a political commitment to make amends. With the camera turned off, he spent half an hour attacking Prime Minister John Howard's conservatism, giving the impression that he, Ruddock, a member of Amnesty, was different. As subsequent events were to demonstrate, not least Amnesty's decision to cancel his membership, this was false.

During the run-up to the 2000 Olympics, the Howard Government was clearly terrified that the outside world would discover hidden, black Australia. With just over a year to go, the United Nations Committee on the Elimination of Racial Discrimination distinguished Australia with its first adverse finding on racial discrimination against a western nation.[16] Added to the numerous Amnesty reports, the opprobrium was beginning to sound like that directed against apartheid South Africa. After enjoying a recently minted reputation as a truly multicultural democracy, far removed from the country's redneck image in the days of the 'White Australia policy', there was cause for concern.

Like Britain and the US, Australia is a single-ideology state with two competing factions, discernible largely by the personalities of their politicians. The difference between Howard's conservative coalition and the opposition Labor Party is that Howard's policies are not veiled. The Labor governments of the 1980s and early 1990s oversaw the greatest redistribution of wealth in the country's history: from bottom to top. They were Thatcherite and Reaganite in all but name. Indeed, Tony Blair described then Prime Minister Paul Keating as his 'inspiration'.

When John Howard came to office in 1996, his first act was to cut $A400 million from the Aboriginal affairs budget – which he referred to contemptuously as the 'Aboriginal industry'. 'Political correctness', as the new Prime Minister put it, had 'gone too far'. There should be 'a new spirit of freedom of expression'. Few doubted the real meaning of his words. He was speaking in Queensland, a state whose historic racism had, in the late nineties, demonstrated its resilience in the election to Federal Parliament of Pauline Hanson as an independent candidate, on an anti-Aboriginal, anti-immigration platform.[17] Her Oxley electorate had one of the highest unemployment rates in Australia. More than half the young people could not find work. Having identified the scapegoats, she made the time-honoured connections. Most importantly, she promoted herself as 'just a naive, hard-working mother' who spoke 'on behalf of the ordinary, average person who's fed up with the pollies [politicians]'. That refrain had a resonance in a country where cynicism about dissembling politicians and their rich 'mates' may be more prevalent than in any western democracy. Hanson said the Aborigines were 'privileged' and that 'millions' were spent on them to no avail. She maintained, in a book written for her, that they 'killed and ate their women and children and occasionally their men'.[18]

This was Howard's opportunity. Apart from calling Hanson an 'empty populist', he pointedly refused to criticise her. In truth, her message was his; only the language was adjusted. Her 'One Nation Party' bore every resemblance to his 'One Australia Policy' which, he had promised in 1988, would be pursued by a future government led by him.

Once in office, Howard began to reverse the most significant gain made by the Aboriginal people. This was the Native Title Act, passed by Federal Parliament in 1993. Based on a landmark ruling by the Australian High Court the year before, the new law had removed from common law the fiction that Australia was uninhabited when Captain James Cook planted the Union flag in 1770. Known as *Terra*

Nullius, it was used for most of two centuries to justify the dispossession of the indigenous population.

Unlike Australia's sheep, the Aborigines were not counted until the late sixties. 'We occupied the land, but we were fauna,' said Aboriginal lawyer Noel Pearson.[19] When British nuclear scientists were given permission by Prime Minister Robert Menzies to test nuclear weapons on Aboriginal land at Maralinga in the 1950s, they used site maps marked 'Uninhabited'. Patrick Connolly, who served with the Royal Air Force at Maralinga, was threatened with prosecution by the security services after he revealed that 'during the two-and-a-half years I was there, I would have seen 400 to 500 Aborigines in contaminated areas. Occasionally, we would bring them in for decontamination. Other times we just shooed them off like rabbits.'[20]

The 1992 High Court judgement, known as the 'Mabo decision', after a successful land rights claimant, Eddie Mabo, was not the victory it was hailed to be at the time. It was a 'historical compromise' between the powerful and the powerless. The judges did not order stolen land to be handed back to native Australians. In deciding that Aborigines might have title to 'crown land' where they had lived continuously, the judges added an escape clause. Land rights could be 'extinguished' by the existence of freeholds and leaseholds held by the huge pastoral estates, many of which the sons of nineteenth-century English aristocrats had acquired, merely by 'squatting' on them.

The Native Title legislation that followed the Mabo judgement was the 'personal mission', as he put it, of the then Labor Prime Minister, Paul Keating, whose speeches about 'reconciliation' reached rhetorical peaks unscaled by his predecessors. Keating's achievement was to sell the critical ambiguity of Mabo to 'moderate'

Aboriginal leaders. It was, he told them, the best deal they would ever get from the white man. Noel Pearson, one of the Aboriginal negotiators, said ruefully, 'To refuse to play the game no longer seemed smart.'[21]

Keating was not slow in showing how the game was played. In accepting his assurances, Aborigines gave up the right of veto over 'development' on much of their land, a fundamental principle of land rights. The Keating Government's unspoken agenda was to confirm the 'land rights' of the mining lobby, promising to hand back to the states the right to 'validate' all Aboriginal land claims. This policy had been central to the strategy of the previous government, led by Bob Hawke, in which Keating had been Treasurer. It was articulated by the then Minister for Resources and Energy, Gareth Evans, who summed it up with what he called 'the three s's'. These were that mining should not be *stopped* on Aboriginal land and the mining companies should not be *'stuffed around'* and *'screwed'* by claims for compensation and royalty payments to Aboriginal communities.[22]

Prime Minister Howard went further. He demanded that Aboriginal communities give up even the right to negotiate land development. His adviser, Queensland Senator Nick Minchen, used code familiar to black Australians, and one echoed by Pauline Hanson. If Aborigines got 'too much', he said, the 'community' would resent their 'special rights' and this would 'undermine the reconciliation process'.[23] In the meantime, the 'pastoralists' and their lobbyists clamoured for the new legislation to be tested. They did not have to wait long. In 1996, in an appeal case involving the Wik people in Queensland, the High Court ruled that Native Title was not necessarily cancelled by a leasehold. In other words, a lease was a lease: it granted possession of the land only for a specific period of time.

Thunderous abuse rained down on the 'radical' and 'politically motivated' judges, from Cabinet ministers, agribusiness, mining groups and their media allies. 'In other circumstances,' wrote the historian Henry Reynolds, 'conservative politicians and business leaders would have flocked to the opposite side of the argument. They would normally applaud the centuries-old battle of the common law to protect property rights against the state. The problem in the Wik case was that the wrong people had acquired rights to the land. What they baulk at is that they will have to deal with indigenous Australians as equals for the first time in 200 years.'[24]

This is the heart of it. 'Most Aborigines,' said the *Canberra Times*, 'gain no legal rights from the Mabo or Wik decisions. What they did gain was a significant moral victory . . . Aboriginal groups have [since] behaved with more dignity and more reason, and more willingness to discuss, negotiate and compromise, than some of the groups still unable to get over the outrage that Aborigines have any rights to land at all.'[25]

That Aborigines had no rights to their own land was a given. In 1896, the Chief Protector of Aborigines in Queensland wrote:

> It seems well to consider our debtors' account with the Aboriginals. Queensland has so far alienated about 10,000,000 acres of freehold land, and leasehold about 300,000,000 for pastoral occupation. For this we have received about six and quarter millions [of pounds] in cash, and for the leasehold land we receive about £332,000 annual rent. Since 1859, we have not expended £50,000 for the benefit of the Aboriginals, and have never since then or before paid them a single shilling in cash, clothes or food, or even an acre of land.[26]

According to a study by Martin Taylor:

> . . . sections of the Queensland pastoral industry participated in the genocide of the Aboriginal people. By 1920, the indigenous people had been reduced from at least 120,000 to 20,000; this involved at least 10,000 direct killings . . . Brutalised Aborigines from the south were imported to form the Queensland Native Police, which was used as a death squad against Aborigines. Disease also ravaged the population.[27]

Considering the received wisdoms of the time, which are shared by many Australians today, none of this was surprising. One of the most widely read textbooks in Queensland schools in the second half of the twentieth century was *Triumph in the Tropics*. Commissioned in 1959 for the state's centenary celebrations, it was the work of Sir Ralph Cilento and Clem Lack. The latter was public relations adviser to the Premier of Queensland. This is one of its references to Aborigines:

> Like his own half-wild dogs, the black could be frozen into shivering immobility or put to frenzied flight by people or things that provoked impressions of terror; or moved to yelps of delight or to racing round, or striking grotesque poses, or to expressing frantic excitement by any sort of clowning . . . In his bushland home he lived in such insecurity that his immediate response to any situation of surprise was almost a conditioned reflex – instantaneous: to strike, to leap aside, to strike, to leap aside, to fall and roll. Like his dogs, too, he could be cowed by a direct and confident stare into a wary

armed truce, but would probably attack with fury if an opponent showed signs of fear, or ran away, or fell disabled. These are primitive reactions common to many feral jungle creatures.[28]

In my experience, a guilt about what has been done to and taken from the native people is deep within the Australian psyche. As I learned when I met a group of relatively liberal-minded pastoralists in Queensland, it is often those with a powerful attachment to the land itself who are most aware that the land is not 'theirs' and that the indigenous people have a unique relationship with it. They told me that their parents and forebears could not have held or managed the land during periods of environmental hardship, such as prolonged drought, without the support of the Aboriginal community. Camilla Cowley, who holds 22,000 acres, said, 'We knew, but we didn't know; the Aborigines were invisible. As a kid, I didn't even lay eyes on one. It only later occurred to me that there weren't any Aboriginal children at my primary school, and the sporting events I went to, because they weren't allowed . . . and yet their knowledge of everything we had to learn in the bush was deeper. My husband was taught to ride a horse by his Aboriginal nanny.'[29]

Without Aboriginal stockmen, some of the largest and most profitable properties would not have survived. These men were paid, at best, half the wages of white workers, plus 'rations'. Their pay went into savings accounts held by the state-owned Commonwealth Bank. They were issued with passbooks, which were held by the local Aboriginal Protector, usually a 'reserve' manager, mission superintendent or policeman. They could not withdraw even the smallest amount without the custodian's agreement, and because many were illiterate they were unable to read the amounts deposited and withdrawn.

Rodney Hall, who was the editor of an Aboriginal newsletter in Queensland in the 1960s, estimates that the sums owed to Aborigines, after a lifetime's work, could amount to millions of dollars. 'These stockmen quite reasonably expected their savings to be accumulating,' he wrote, 'but the balance seldom amounted to more than a few thousand dollars, sometimes just a few hundred . . . [I] alerted the media, [but there was] never an answer. Never a single letter or phone call from a mainstream newspaper, radio or television station. Not one. The issue was not allowed to exist in the national forum. Somebody's pockets were lined. Are we to believe it was the protectors? Or the holders of the pastoral leases? Once this has been cleared up, we can revisit the subject of the scale of reparations Aboriginal people may legitimately expect.'[30]

The scale of reparations might be calculated against a historical truth which no Australian government has acknowledged. In 1837, a House of Commons Select Committee conducted an investigation into the conditions of native peoples in the British colonies. Only one people was found to have been denied absolutely the right of prior ownership of their land: the Australian Aborigines. The Select Committee's report was unequivocal. The first Australians had 'an incontrovertible right to their own soil, a plain and sacred right, however, which seems not to have been understood . . . The land has been taken from them without the assertion of any other title other than that of superior force.'[31]

This was also the view of the British government. The Colonial Office in London had created pastoral leases with one aim: to ensure that Aborigines would continue to have access to their land although it was leased to 'squatters'. The policy was not meant as a source of enrichment for whites, but as compensation to the Aborigines for the annexation and colonisation of their land. 'The pastoral lease policy was the high point of British humanitarian concern,' wrote the historian Henry Reynolds. 'The present Australian government is offering the Aborigines less than the British imperial authorities 150 years ago.'[32]

The 'less' is epitomised by John Howard's Native Title Amendment Act of 1998, which waters down the 1993 law, wipes out the universal principle of Native Title in all but name and takes away the common law rights that the judges said belonged to Aborigines; nothing like it has been passed by a modern parliament anywhere. The beneficiaries are not small white farmers, frightened by government propaganda depicting a 'black tide' engulfing properties and lapping the family barbie, but some of the richest and most powerful companies and individuals in white Australia.

Potentially, 42 per cent of Australia could pass from leasehold to freehold land controlled by fewer than 20,000 people, including those with the most influential media and political connections. They include Kerry Packer, owner of the Nine national television network, who is the seventh largest landholder in the country, and Rupert Murdoch, who controls 70 per cent of the capital city press and owns nine vast properties. The two top private landholders, Hugh McLachlan and the McDonald family, both have close ties with the National Party, Howard's coalition partners.

In essence, Howard's law means the expropriation from one group of Australians, the indigenous people, of property rights that the High Court has said are theirs, the object being to advantage another group, all of whom happen to be white and wealthy. Right down to its obfuscating detail, the new law is reminiscent of those enacted by the apartheid regime in South Africa. It was this that the UN Committee for the Elimination of Racial Discrimination condemned, with one committee member describing the law as 'a sweeping disinvestment of native title rights'.[33]

The result has been legal attrition, as the new regulations are interpreted differently from state to state, leaving Aborigines in a catch-22 of having to prove their 'continuous connection' with lands of which they have been dispossessed. In the state of Victoria, the claim of the 4,500 Yorta Yorta people to their traditional homelands was rejected by a judge, who based his decision on the amended law, having heard from a powerful array of white political and corporate interests. The claim reached back to the 1850s when white authorities typically tried to detribalise and Christianise the Yorta Yorta, often violently. Families and clans were broken up, as men and women were sent to a lifetime of peonage and children to 'training homes'. 'The Yorta Yorta faced an epic task,' wrote Katrina Alford of LaTrobe University, Melbourne. 'They were required to prove their traditional connection with the lands claimed, on both geographical and genealogical grounds, and to present this evidence in a legally acceptable written form – difficult at the best of times, but almost impossible for native title claimants with an oral tradition.' She quoted the historian Patrick Wolfe: 'The more you have lost, the less you stand to gain. To fall within Native Title criteria, it is necessary to fall outside history.'[34]

In 1997, the Australian Human Rights and Equal Opportunity Commission released a damning and painful report, *Bringing Them Home*, on perhaps the darkest chapter in the nation's history: that of the 'stolen generation'.[35] It described how thousands of Aboriginal children of mixed race were taken from their parents as part of a systematic policy in order to 'breed out the colour'.[36] Police were used to find and steal children. They had orders not to tell them or their parents where they were being taken. Describing one such 'heartrending scene', the *Sydney Morning Herald* reported, on January 10, 1925:

> The separation occurred just before Christmas . . . It appeared that a police officer's instructions were to meet the parents at the ferry, and thither [the children] went accompanied by their parents, who did not know that their little ones were to be taken away from them. The scene at the parting was heartrending, but the children were taken, despite protests and tears . . . The parents were in a terrible state about it . . .

As previously suppressed files now reveal, there was often no pretence of taking into care 'neglected' children, who were stolen from loving families. Robert T Donaldson, an inspector of the perversely named Aborigines Protection Board, became infamous as the 'kids collector': a gaunt figure who roamed New South Wales, appearing with sweets and disappearing with children.

The policy was inspired by the fascist eugenics movement, which was fashionable in the first two decades of the twentieth century and spread the fear that white women were not breeding fast enough and the 'white race' would be 'swamped'. During the 1930s, this was known as 'assimilation' and was promoted by the Professor of Anthropology at Sydney University, AP Elkin, who speculated that Aborigines were the 'lowest race' and 'parasites' that should be 'absorbed'.[37] The boys were sent to sheep and cattle stations as labourers and paid in rations and pennies. The girls, who were the majority, were sent mostly to the

Cootamundra Training Home for Aboriginal Girls, where they were trained to be domestic servants, then 'indentured' to 'masters' in white middle-class homes. The historic parallel is with the use of black slave girls as domestics in the American southern states before Emancipation.

While books, plays and laments have been written about the dispossession and suffering of black Americans, there has been only a tentative recognition in Australia. For many years, a popular belief was that the children were being 'saved' from the horrors of a 'primitive' upbringing, in particular the 'half-castes' — when, in fact, many were abused and most received no protection from the state. Some white Australians professed ignorance of these crimes; it seems the majority met them with indifference and silence.

The President of the Human Rights Commission, Sir Ronald Wilson, said, 'We as a committee have decided that what was done meets the international definition of genocide . . . which is the attempt to destroy a people, a culture.' *Bringing Them Home*, the commission's report, called for an official apology on behalf of all Australians. John Howard has steadfastly refused to make this single gesture, let alone to consider compensation. During the week the report was tabled, Federal Parliament spent an hour debating a proposal for a tax on the culling of emus. By contrast, *Bringing Them Home*, which described genocide in Australia, was given half an hour, during which the Prime Minister, the members of his Cabinet and most government MPs left the chamber before the 'debate' was over.

I am of the age of many of the stolen generation. Like most whites, I grew up playing the subconscious role of innocent bystander in my own country. When I entered high school, a standard history textbook was *Man Makes History: World History from the Earliest Times to the Renaissance* by Russel Ward. It sold more than 200,000 copies and said this:

> Boys and girls often ask, 'What's the use of history?'
> Answer: There are still living today in Arnhem Land people who know almost no history. They are Aboriginal tribesmen who live in practically the same way as their forefathers and ours did, tens of thousands of years ago . . . We are civilised today and they are not. History helps us to understand why this is so.[38]

The standard Australian atlas in circulation from 1939 to 1966 described white 'exploration' of Australia as 'the curtain of darkness . . . being slowly rolled back'. The areas of 'explored' Australia were represented as white oases in an otherwise dark continent.[39] As *Triumph in the Tropics* had pointed out, Australia was an 'empty land' because its inhabitants did not count as humans. They were part of the fauna. And as such they possessed no rights, nor any claim to morality; and the Christian gentlemen who chronicled the Australian story were very keen on morality. A 1970 reprint of *The Squatting Age in Australia* by Professor Stephen Roberts concluded that: 'It was quite useless to treat [the Aborigines] fairly, since they were completely amoral and usually incapable of sincere and prolonged gratitude.'[40]

Wally MacArthur is one of the stolen generation. Taken from his mother as a small boy, he grew up in the Bungalow mission near

Alice Springs, which his close friend, Charlie Perkins, the great activist who also grew up there, described as 'a concentration camp in the bush'.[41] As a 'half-caste', Wally was destined to be a servant of some kind in white society. He had one outstanding gift: he could run fast. Those who have studied Wally's times believe he was one of the fastest athletes of all time, the Carl Lewis of his day. At the age of fourteen, and running without shoes, he broke every record for a schoolboy and was declared 'the fastest fourteen-year-old in the world'.

He was known as the Borroloola Flash, after Borroloola, a speck of a place on the MacArthur River. 'That's how I got my name actually,' he told me. 'They didn't know my name when they took me away from my mum, and down to Alice Springs. The government, you know, took me away . . .'

'How old were you?'

'I must have been about six. But when I got to Alice Springs, I was a bit of a comic strip, because I couldn't understand the language; I couldn't speak English. I was still speaking my native language. It wasn't too bad; you were allowed to roam around on the edge of the Todd River.'

'What happened to your parents?'

'I just lost contact with them altogether. When I did go back after fifty-five years, I met my younger brother and he was only about eight or nine months when I left, when they took me away. When we met again, it was great. We hugged one another, we cried. It was a funny experience, because we got on the booze and he got me drunk and the next day, I apologised to the elders. I said in pidgin English to them, "I been sorry, you elders. I been getting my brother drunk. He been miss work." And they said, "No, it's all right, Wally, you don't have to worry; we're happy that you come and see your brother. Anyway, it's the only time he ever drank. He doesn't drink." That was the only time in his life he drank a drop.'

'Do you remember the day you were taken away?'

'Yes, I remember very well. It was a government car, because only the government had cars at that time. The driver put me in the front seat with him and he drove around while I waved at my family. I never seen them since, you know. They were sitting around the campfire; they didn't understand what was happening, I bet. I was taken into Mataranka where the railway station was, and I was shipped off to Darwin.'

'Did you miss your family?'

'Well, I thought I was going on a holiday, you see . . . But when I missed them, I wanted to get back, but I couldn't.'

'Who discovered you could run?'

'Well, once a year, the kids at the Bungalow [mission] were taken into Alice Springs for an athletics carnival, sort of. I used to run in everything and win them all. All in bare feet. For my first win, I got a bent shilling. I won a lot of races after that, but I could never get into the state team. So I decided to turn pro. I ran against the Australian professional champion, Frank Banner. He gave me four yards start, and I beat him by six . . . It was then that a talent scout from the English rugby league club the Rochdale Hornets asked me if I'd like to go to England and play on the wing.

'When I arrived in London, one of the papers there had a headline, "Black Flash on the way", and I thought, "Gee, I'm not that black, am I?" I got the train straight up to Manchester. The next day, the *Manchester News* had the headline: "Coffee-coloured Aussie arrives". I thought, "Gee, I've gone from being black to coffee-coloured." But I didn't care, because people in England loved the Borroloola Flash. They used to say: "The Flash does it again." I loved that. I still hold the record for scoring 38 points in one game. I was the fastest winger they'd ever seen. They couldn't catch me, you see.'[42]

Australia's hidden history is Aboriginal. Few in my sports-obsessed country know that the first Australian cricket team to tour England was entirely black. That was 1868, a decade before the first white touring team. The *Daily Telegraph* mused, 'Nothing of interest comes from Australia except gold nuggets and black cricketers.' *The Times* described the black Australians as 'perfectly civilised, and quite familiar with the English language'.[43]

Like Wally MacArthur, Eddie Gilbert is another forgotten name. In the 1930s, Eddie, a fast bowler, was given special permission to play outside the Queensland reserve, in a white team. He took five wickets for sixty-five runs against the West Indies. In 1931, he faced Donald Bradman, the world's greatest batsman, and bowled him for a duck. Bradman later wrote, 'He sent down in that period the fastest "bowling" I can remember . . . one delivery knocked the bat out of my hand and I unhesitatingly class this short burst faster than anything seen from [Harold] Larwood or anyone else.'[44] Historian Thom Blake wrote that 'the occasion demonstrated that the black could triumph over white. Living on the settlement, inmates were constantly reminded of their inferior status as blacks . . . Bradman's dismissal gave inmates a sense of hope and pride [which] countered the usual stereotypes of Aborigines as lazy, useless primitives.'[45]

On November 11, 1936, the Secretary of the Queensland Cricket Association wrote to the Protector of Aborigines, 'The matter of Eddie Gilbert has been fully discussed by my executive committee and it was decided, with your concurrence, to arrange for Gilbert to return to the settlement . . . With regard to the cricketing clothes bought for Gilbert, it is asked that arrangements be made for these to be laundered, and delivery of the laundered clothes to be made to this office.' His cricketing whites were duly collected by the Fish Steam Laundry on November 16, 1936.[46] Thus they solved the problem of a remarkable sportsman who dared to be too good for his own good.

Later, suffering from alcoholism and a degenerative brain disorder, Eddie Gilbert was committed to a mental asylum, where he spent twenty-three years, often mistreated. He died there. This was a common way of dealing with uppity blacks, especially those afflicted with 'the grog'. They would be committed to an institution by the Chief Protector, for 'such time as he shall think fit'.

Charlie Samuels was a phenomenal Aboriginal sprinter who ran a hundred yards in 9.10 seconds in 1888, which was faster than the disqualified Ben Johnson at the Seoul Olympics a hundred years later. When he stopped winning races, Charlie was sent to Callan Park Lunatic Asylum in Sydney. The admission form said he was suffering from 'ill health and love affairs'. In fact, like so many Aboriginal people, he was desperately ill. After the Chief Protector had banished his wife and two children, he was sent to a reserve in Queensland, where he died alone.[47]

The great Aboriginal boxer Ron Richards died a prisoner on Palm Island reserve, off the coast of Queensland. Richards was Australian middleweight, light-heavyweight and heavyweight champion and British Empire middleweight champion. 'Like many another Crossbreeds of his race,' wrote the Chief Protector in 1935, 'he is unstable in character and inclined to be gullible.'[48]

Wally MacArthur's childhood mate, Charlie Perkins, was born on a table-top in a disused telegraph station near Alice Springs in 1936 or 1937; he was not sure which. When we first met, Charlie told me about his brother, no doubt as a way of telling me something about himself. Like many 'half-castes', he had killed himself after a short life, described by Charlie as 'trying non-stop to win the recognition and respect of whites'.

'You learned from when you were a little kid,' he said, 'that you kept out of the way of whites. At the mission, our big treat was being taken to the pictures, sneaking in after the movie had started and leaving before it ended, so that no one would object to us black kids being there. I grew up never knowing if the goodies or baddies won. Very frustrating.'

Charlie's mother, Hetti, was a 'dormitory girl' at the Bungalow mission, near Alice Springs. Charlie believes he was never stolen because Hetti never took her eyes off him. 'She carried me on her back,' he said, 'or she watched me like a hawk when there were coppers or government people around, inspecting the place.'[49]

Charlie never saw a football until he was sent to a missionary secondary school in Adelaide. 'I reckon my foot connected with the ball as the most natural thing in the world,' he said. 'It was a wonderful feeling to discover what you're good at.' At sixteen, he was spotted by a talent scout for the Merseyside club Everton, who offered to pay half his fare to England. He went, arriving midway through the season in a freezing winter. 'I had my ups and downs with Everton. The pitches were as hard as rock, but I was determined to make a go of it.' Offered a transfer to a first-division club by Matt Busby of Manchester United, he holds the distinction of turning the great man down. 'I had found a kind of racial peace in England,' he said, 'but I was homesick, and I wanted to play in my own country.'

Charlie returned home to all the ambivalence that consumes many Aboriginal people. 'I was so pleased to be back,' he said, 'seeing that wonderful light, hearing the birds, seeing my mates, but I felt the racism more than ever. For one thing, no white person ever invited me home for a meal, for anything. Lucky for me, Sydney soccer was mostly a migrants' game, and I played for clubs whose players were mostly non-English-speaking immigrants. Among the Yugoslavs and the Greeks,' he said, 'I found more acceptance of me as an Australian than among my own. I was an outsider from the inside: very confusing.'

He became only the second Aborigine to graduate from an Australian university. In the mid-sixties, he began to make his name as a 'troublemaker' when he led white students on 'freedom rides' into the outback of New South Wales. Their objective was much the same as that of the freedom riders who began the desegregation of the Deep South in the United States. Abused, spat at and physically attacked, they went to places where 'nigger hunts' were still not uncommon. They stood at the turnstiles of local pools, sports fields and cinemas and demanded an end to the race bar. 'At Moree, I thought we'd had it,' he told me, 'then this black woman stepped forward and made a courageous speech in which she pointed to a white man who had gone secretly with black women and fathered black children. "Tell your wives what you've been doing, you bludgers!" she said. "Go on, they're just over there: tell 'em!" That evening black kids were allowed into the pool for the first time.

'There was a real significance about that victory, because this being Australia, sport and other people's wars are the national pastimes. That's why, going right back in time, country towns, which had lousy housing and rotten schools, would have great sporting facilities, athletics tracks and cricket and football ovals and marvellous Olympic-standard swimming pools. Letting blacks into the pool was crossing a threshold; it couldn't ever be allowed. In that way, we were just like South Africa. Here, blacks weren't even allowed in the grandstands – not even in a blacks-only section. The whole area of sporting activity was banned to us. The only time we got in was when some compassionate church person or an athletics official felt that you had so much talent you couldn't possibly be excluded. But as soon as you'd reached their expectations, and began to fade, mostly they didn't want to know you. I'm not saying there weren't any really good ones; but mostly they walked away. All of our Aboriginal sporting stars played under that kind of pressure, knowing that when their careers finished, they were finished. Look at the great fighter, Lionel Rose. He got a ticker-tape parade when he won the world title, then when he lost, they dumped him so hard he went on the grog and never recovered. He became just another black.

'That's why lots of Aboriginal sporting people didn't declare themselves as Aborigines. A bit swarthy, they could get away with it: like Clive Churchill, the great rugby league player who was captain of Australia. Today, there's two people in the Australian side I know are Aborigines, but they won't declare themselves. They're too scared. There are lots like that in this country. I'd say that 90 per cent of old white families have some Aboriginal blood. That's one of the reasons they've turned so viciously against us.

'In South Africa, at least you knew where you stood. In Australia, you can have a friend and an enemy all in one person, especially if you're like me, of mixed blood. You know what I mean? Someone who will call you his mate one minute, then before you know it, you feel an indifference, a coldness you can't explain. The thing is you're never sure. It's what drove my brother to kill himself.'

Charlie and I became lifelong friends shortly after the freedom rides when I went beyond the Australian frontier for the first time and saw that which I had never imagined. Charlie was my guide. At Alice Springs, we hired a Ford Falcon and picked up Hetti, his mother, who wore a big black hat; the former dormitory girl was, after all, a queen of the Arrente people. We headed for the government reserve at Jay Creek, where 300 people were corralled without running water or proper food and housing. The barbed-wire gate was locked; a Department of the Interior sign read: 'Prohibited Entry'.

'Do it,' said Hetti.

I reversed the car, revved it and smashed through the gate.

'G'day!' said Charlie to the white manager, whose ablutions we had interrupted.

'Where's your bloody permit?'

'Lost it, mate.'

Today, Jay Creek has no barbed wire and there is an ablution block and houses of a kind, and no one needs a permit. But the third-world poverty remains, along with an insidious control, imposed by deprivation and the law. This is the Northern Territory, where a sixteen-year-old Aboriginal boy was left hanging all night in his cell and another Aboriginal teenager was sent to prison for a year for stealing a towel (which he had returned). At Jay Creek, there is still nowhere to play a proper game of sport. When they were considering Sydney's bid, the International Olympic Committee ought to have seen places like this, or at least read Colin Tatz's remarkable book, *Obstacle Race: Aborigines in Sport*.

Until his recent retirement, Tatz was professor of politics at Sydney's Macquarie University, where he established one of only three academic centres in the world devoted to genocide studies. A South African political refugee, he found in Australia echoes of his own country. 'People say to me,' he said, 'surely, South Africa was an example of dreadful maniacal, premeditated racism where Australia was really a case of innocent ignorance. The truth is there is a tremendous similarity, both in ideology and notions of scientific racial theories: for example, the fuller the blood, the more primitive, the lighter the skin colour, the more salvageable. The reserves, the exploitative labour, the sexual exploitation of women, the separate health systems, the separate education, the ban on interracial marriage – all are the same.'

Obstacle Race is the secret history of Aboriginal sport and its achievements, which, says Tatz, 'are little short of miraculous'. Of the 1,200 black sportsmen and women he studied, only six had access to the same sporting facilities and opportunities as whites. His book is a moving testament to the endeavours of the first Australians to live up to the sports-obsessed culture of the majority. He describes the dustbowls, and the fields of mud and salt and strewn rock where black Australian athletes have trained and played, and won through, often against the odds of their fragile health. There is a photograph of the Rovers rugby league team, in Ceduna, the 1958 champions. Most died in their thirties and forties.

Tatz has little time for the 'Olympic spirit we all share', which he regards as fraudulent. 'The IOC sent out its special representative, a Nigerian,' he said. 'His assignment was to examine conditions here: to see if we were a fit and proper country to have the Olympics. What he was interested in was discrimination in sport, but he saw nothing, because he wasn't taken anywhere. I believe he would have been shocked to the marrowbones had he gone to places like Yuendumu in the Northern Territory where there is an annual Aboriginal games of great significance, where there isn't a blade of grass, where there isn't a set of goal posts, where there isn't a basketball court, where words like coach and track and pools and physios and scholarships are just not part of the Aboriginal vocabulary.

'On the salt pan at Lombadina, Aborigines play with two saplings stuck in the ground. If he had inspected these conditions, he would have been looking at third- and fourth-world sporting facilities. He would have seen Aborigines kicking a piece of leather stuffed with paper because they don't possess a single football or have access to the kind of sports facilities that every white Australian takes for granted, even in poor working-class suburbs where there is a municipal pool, a municipal ground, a cricket pitch or a tennis court or a park of some sort – these things are totally absent in 95 per cent of Aboriginal communities.'

I asked him if white Australians were aware of this.

'Australians don't want their fun spoiled by social reality, but it's fair to say most would weep if they were taken on a tour of black sporting Australia. There is a great push to have more and more Aboriginal athletes, more and more scholarships for an elite group of sports people, because it will be wonderful to say in the Olympics year: "Look, we have half-a-dozen Aborigines in our briefcases, which shows that Australia makes no racial distinctions and everybody lives happily in a land of equal opportunity." But the Aborigines who represent Australia in the Olympics had to show three times as much talent in order to rate an equal place with whites. Cathy Freeman is the greatest thing that ever happened to white Australia because this happy, delightful, fun-loving young lady looks as though she is the representative of all black woman-hood, and she is not; she is an aberration.'[50]

In 1998, Tatz published a monograph, *Genocide in Australia*, in which he argued that, under international convention, Australia is guilty of at least two types of genocide:

> Firstly, the essentially private genocide, the physical killing, committed by settlers and rogue police officers in the nineteenth century, while the state, in the form of the colonial authorities, stood silently by (for the most part); secondly, the twentieth century official state policy and practice of forcibly transferring children from one group to another with the express intention they cease being Aboriginal.

He quotes the Chief Protector in Western Australia, CF Gale: 'I would not hesitate for one moment to separate any half-caste from its Aboriginal mother, no matter how frantic her momentary grief might be at the time. They soon forget their offspring.' Very few Australians, wrote Tatz,

> . . . use the word [genocide]. Almost all historians of the Aboriginal experience – black or white – avoid it. They write about pacifying, killing, cleansing, excluding, exterminating, starving, poisoning, shooting, beheading, sterilising, exiling, removing – but avoid genocide. Are they ignorant of genocide theory and practice? Or simply reluctant to taint 'the land of fair go', the 'lucky country', with so heinous a label?

And he reminds Australians that, in acts of genocide, 'there are three parties: the perpetrators, the victims – and the bystanders.'[51]

When Sir Ronald Wilson, the former High Court judge who

chaired the *Bringing Them Home* inquiry, used the word 'genocide', he was accused of 'intemperate slander' and roundly abused by government politicians and the far-right commentators who dominate the Australian press.[52] Like Colin Tatz and a few other bravehearts, he had broken white Australia's most enduring taboo. Central to this is the suppression of Aboriginal population figures; for if historians were to reveal that large numbers of people inhabited the 'empty land' at the time of the invasion, the deduction would have to be made that the genocide was on an even more appalling scale than had been previously assessed.

On the eve of the bicentenary of white settlement in 1988, a sensational 'discovery' was made by the anthropologist Dr Peter White and Australia's most celebrated pre-historian, Professor DJ Mulvaney. They reported that the Aboriginal population in 1788 was 750,000, or three times the previous estimate. They concluded that more than 600,000 people had died in the years following the invasion. News of this was published on page sixteen of the *Sydney Morning Herald* under the byline of the paper's 'Environment Writer'.[53]

The Mulvaney/White disclosure was supported by the new historiography of Henry Reynolds, Ross Fitzgerald, Noel Butlin and others, who literally wrote the Aboriginal story on to the blank pages of Australia's history, until then a faintly heroic tale of the white man struggling against nature, of 'national achievement' devoid of blacks, women and other complicating factors. With the Aborigines included, the narrative was completely different. It was a story of theft, dispossession and warfare, of massacre and resistance. It was a story every bit as rapacious as those of the United States, Spanish America and colonial Africa and Asia. It was, above all, a political story.

In breaking the silence, these historians incurred the wrath of an influential group of white supremacists, including Prime Minister John Howard. These are the '*Quadrant* denialists'; *Quadrant* is a far-right magazine deployed in a manner not dissimilar to the way David Irving used his history texts to promote Holocaust denial. They reject the 'black armband view of history', an expression coined by the Australian historian Geoffrey Blainey, who now appears to have disowned it. 'Black armband' historians, say the denialists, denigrate the heroic story of white Australia by the manufacture and exaggeration of evidence of Aboriginal suffering and resistance. Genocide simply did not happen, they say.

Australia is a country littered with war memorials to its Anzac soldiers who died in foreign wars. There was, until recently, not a single monument to those who fought and fell in defence of their country, Australia, during its invasion and occupation in the eighteenth and nineteenth centuries. The late Kevin Gilbert, the great Aboriginal poet and playwright, once stood in the main street of a New South Wales country town, facing the cenotaph, and read aloud his poem *Memorials*:

> Our history is carved
> in the heart of the country
> our milestone memorials
> named Slaughterhouse Creek
> the Coniston Massacre, Death
> Gully and Durranurrijah
> the place on the clifftops called
> Massacre Leap
> where the mouth of the valley
> filled up with

> our murdered dead bodies
> the place where our blood flowed
> the river ran red
> all the way to the sea . . .

In 1998, John Howard dismissed the idea that the Australian National War Memorial in Canberra should recognise Aborigines killed in frontier conflict because, he said, a state of war never existed. 'How then,' asks Henry Reynolds, 'are we to account for the dead? If the 20,000 and more Aborigines were not killed in a long-drawn-out sporadic warfare, they must have been murdered. There does not seem to be any other alternative . . . [They] must have been murdered by soldiers, policemen and by the settlers themselves . . . The whole of colonial society was complicit in the killing, with governments and courts failing on a massive scale to enforce the law and bring the killers to justice. Why we should consider this as a more acceptable way of seeing frontier conflict, rather than viewing it as a kind of warfare, is hard to imagine.' He pointed out that, had 20,000 settlers died defending their country against invaders, the 'important sites of conflict throughout the country would be located, listed and marked appropriately'.[54]

Unlike in the United States, South Africa and New Zealand, no such sites are marked and commemorated. In Australia, there were no more than 'a few skirmishes on the frontier', according to Federal minister Philip Ruddock. His Cabinet colleague, Minister for Aboriginal Affairs John Herron, went further, contending that only one in ten Aboriginal children was 'removed' and there was no 'stolen generation'. When the Aboriginal elder Lowitja O'Donoghue said she preferred to describe herself as 'removed' rather than 'stolen', right-wing commentators joined with the

Prime Minister in further diminishing the 'stolen generation'. In announcing that there had been no killings in Tasmania, a state renowned for its extermination policies, the former Premier, Ray Broom, became, in Colin Tatz's words, 'Australia's foremost genocide denialist in the 1990s'.[55]

In contrast to any other democracy, the participation of the Prime Minister in this revisionism has given the denial campaign significance and popular profile. It is the equivalent of the President of the United States questioning the truth of slavery. In supporting an enclave of journalists, academics and politicians, similar to the Australian McCarthyites of the 1950s, Howard gave a certain respectability to the group's attack on the report *Bringing Them Home*, whose testimony they described as part of a hoax, a monument to 'false memory syndrome'.[56] Given an airing by windbag-columnists and those who inhabit the netherworld of radio talk-back bigotry, their denial of genocide has celebrated the work of second-rate academics, including one who made the astonishing claim that frontier killings could not possibly have taken place 'because most colonists were Christian to whom such actions were abhorrent'.

Tell that to the native peoples of the Americas, Africa, Asia and Australia. 'Like so many genocide denialists,' wrote Tatz, 'they assert but don't demonstrate, they disapprove but don't ever disprove. Rather, they rely on a "new" methodology: attacking the integrity of authors and witnesses. [Henry] Reynolds, for example, now has "a tattered reputation" and I am a "scare-monger" seeking to impale Australia on exaggerated history. Besides, I'm Jewish with a Holocaust agenda.'[57]

The denialists have had some success. Sir Ronald Wilson, the Human Rights Commissioner, has recanted on his use of the word 'genocide'.[58] From their platforms in the press, they have helped the Howard Government regenerate a xenophobia aimed at helpless people in leaking boats seeking refuge in Australia. Indeed, they can take comfort, says Tatz, 'in their one undisputed achievement – their ability to hurt the victim people'.[59]

The courts and prisons have long been the institutional channels for this cruelty. 'It's an attitude given legitimacy, a green light for the old ways to continue,' the Aboriginal lawyer Michael Mansell told me. 'I've been in courts in the outback of Western Australia where, out of a hundred people, I saw at most one or two whites. All the rest going before the court were Aborigines. In one magistrate's court, an Aboriginal woman who couldn't speak English, and whose legal representative spoke to her for only two minutes before the hearing, was told her child would be taken away from her. She had been drunk; she was ill. I've seen an Aboriginal child taken from his family for stealing a car and sent to an institution for years. This is a legalised version of the old policies that produced the stolen generation. There is no real pressure on the police and the magistrates to think of Aborigines as equal in their humanity to whites. In this political atmosphere, violence and injustice are simply undeterred.'[60]

It is more than twelve years since a Royal Commission into Aboriginal Deaths in Custody heard that Aborigines were the majority in prisons in several states and that they were neglected and, by any definition, tortured; and they killed themselves in their teens. After sitting for two years at a cost of $A30 million, the Commission recommended the blindingly obvious: that Aborigines should be imprisoned only as a last resort.[61] Since then, Aborigines have been sent to prison at a rate higher than ever before and the number dying behind bars has doubled.[62] Michael Mansell says the imprisonment rate of Aborigines and the incidence of their deaths in custody is the highest in the world, higher than in South Africa and the United States. If the same rate was applied to whites in prison, 8,000 would have died in eight years.[63]

I first met Leila and Arthur Murray in 1987, four years to the day since their son, Eddie, had been found hanged in a police station in Wee Waa, a country town in New South Wales. Eddie was a star player with the Redfern All Blacks rugby team and in 1981 was chosen to tour New Zealand. He was, said Arthur, 'a spirited, happy-go-lucky boy with everything to live for'.[64] Eddie's 'spirit' guaranteed that he saw a lot of the police.

The imposing police station at Wee Waa, known to the locals as the 'Opera House', was built in the early seventies when large numbers of Aborigines migrated to the surrounding district, looking for work in the cotton fields. 'There was a nine o'clock curfew for blacks then,' one of them recalled, 'and the whites used to sell blacks metho [methylated spirits] on ice in the liquor store.'[65]

On June 21, 1983, Eddie Murray was arrested and taken to Wee Waa police station. His crime was being drunk. Within an hour, he was dead, strangled with a blanket in his cell. At the coroner's inquest, the police claimed Eddie had killed himself by hanging, even though his blood alcohol level at the time was extremely high. Under cross-examination, the police agreed that Eddie was 'so drunk he couldn't scratch himself'. Yet, according to them, Eddie had managed to tear off a strip of a thick prison blanket, deftly fold it, thread it through the bars of the ventilation window, tie two knots, fashion a noose and hang himself without his feet leaving the ground.

One policeman gave evidence that he was off-duty that day, then admitted he had lied when four Aboriginal witnesses identified him as one of those in the police van that took Eddie away. The coroner was told about witnesses who were not interviewed and serious discrepancies in police notebooks, with dates appearing out of sequence and an absence of records altogether – except for a highly detailed record of the events of June 21, the day of Eddie's arrest and death. The coroner found that Eddie had died 'at the hands of person or persons unknown'. He said there was no evidence that Eddie had taken his own life and he strongly criticised the police. And that was that.

Eddie's parents began a tenacious campaign for justice. They petitioned three New South Wales Attorney-Generals; they described how the police bore a grudge against Eddie for giving evidence against them in a previous case; they wrote letter upon letter to the local hospital, asking for the return of Eddie's clothes, which were never found. Arthur believes there is a political factor; he had made powerful local enemies by organising many of the black cotton workers. 'We want answers; we just want answers,' he said, when we met at the family's home in Marrickville, a poor suburb of Sydney. Leila interrupted, 'They're killing Aboriginal people . . . just killing them.'[66]

In 1997, the Murrays won an important victory. Eddie's body was exhumed, another autopsy was conducted and the coroner cast doubt on the original finding. This time it was found that Eddie had a fractured sternum, which could have been caused by severe blows to the chest up to three days before he died. The Murrays now demanded an independent public inquiry into Eddie's death, and that the Director of Public Prosecutions review all the police testimony.

In 1998, I met Leila and Arthur in the same front room of their Marrickville home. Eddie's pictures were all about, and his football trophies. The Murrays appeared like many Aboriginal people I have known, who have fought the system through the system. Surrounded by wedges of documents, their emotions on the edge, they looked exhausted. 'I don't think I can take any more,' said Leila. 'We need answers . . .'

I asked, 'When do you think things will ever change in this country?'

'Never,' replied Arthur.

'When we get justice,' said Leila, who had begun to cry. 'They owe us this, you know. They owe us for what they took away from us: our son. They talk about reconciliation and all that, and the politicians jump up and down because Sydney got the Olympics. But what does that all come to if there's no justice for Aboriginal people? Why don't they boycott the Olympic Games, you know, stop them? If we can't get justice, why should they have the Olympic Games over here?'[67]

Robert Cavanagh, a barrister and law lecturer who has helped the Murrays prepare their case, was listening to this. 'If Eddie had been young, white and rich,' he said, 'there would have been a wholly different approach taken to his death. There would have been investigators flown in to deal with it at the time. His body would have been removed to an appropriate place for an appropriate autopsy. This was not done. People would have been thoroughly questioned, and there would have been a real attempt to determine how he died. None of that occurred for Eddie. And that was because he was black and poor.'[68]

As the Olympic Games approached, the Federal and New South Wales governments began to show signs of panic. With the opening ceremony three weeks away, the Howard Government responded to yet another damning United Nations report on

Aboriginal health by banning visits by UN human rights inspectors and declaring it would no longer appear before UN human rights committees. The Attorney-General described the issues of discrimination raised by the UN as 'minor, marginal issues'.[69] Australian Olympic Committee officials, who had allowed Aboriginal activists to set up an 'indigenous cultural pavilion' near the main stadium, now demanded they sign a contract banning 'political speeches, demonstrations and marches' on the site during the games. The Director-General of the Olympic Co-ordination Authority, David Richmond, threatened 'sanctions' if the 'special conditions' were contravened and warned that the Authority 'reserves the right to review the text of all material on display other than text describing works of art'.[70]

As a sporting spectacular, the games were a resounding success, thanks largely to thousands of ordinary Australians who signed up as volunteers, and exuded the friendliness that disarms visitors. The highlight, for Australians, was Cathy Freeman's win in the 400 metres. With its Aboriginal heroine, the Australian 'image' seemed safe. 'She united certain emotions,' said Michael Mansell. 'She made the whites feel good and she gave many Aboriginal youngsters a role model. As for the rest of us, trying to tell the world of the truth and shame behind the feelgood, we got some things out, but we were no match for the Olympic juggernaut.'

When the games were over, I looked for Charlie Perkins, who had gone quiet, which was not like him. Instead of leading a 'march of shame', he had slipped into hospital with a cancer that had been threatening him for years. I phoned him at his bedside and asked what on earth he was doing there. 'Listen, mate,' he said, 'I've got to my sixties and, for a blackfella, that's bloody amazing.'

We talked about when he used to come to London and call me

from Heathrow and say, 'Get the journos out, mate. There's a demo in the Strand outside Australia House that will tell the Poms about an Australia that's just like South Africa.'

Knowing his reply, I would ask how many were going.

'Me and you.'

Charlie died the next day, and Sydney stopped for his funeral. He was much admired; he also made plenty of enemies, because he invariably pointed a finger at a white society that could never patronise him. When Sydney University gave him a long-overdue honorary doctorate, he used the occasion to savage the politicians; and now he was dead, they were paying their unctuous tributes to him. Charlie was Australia's Martin Luther King.

Mick Dodson is another Renaissance man, one of a group of sophisticated Aboriginal activists who understand more about white society than it understands itself. A lawyer, he was a Social Justice Commissioner and served on the Royal Commission into deaths in custody. 'They know, the whites know,' he told me, 'that the things that most clearly and distinctively portray Australia to the world are Aboriginal things. They will say, "Well, we'll accept your culture for the showcase, but we hate that Mick Dodson; he's too much of an activist." Or: "We love Cathy Freeman, but we don't like that Charlie Perkins." Or: "We're happy to have your world-renowned Bangara Dance Theatre, but we don't want anything to do with political organisations fighting for land rights. And, by the way, you're not going to make us feel guilty, because it's got nothing to do with this generation." The Prime Minister says that all the time . . . and maybe there was some truth in it a short time ago. I mean, maybe they could claim distance from the past. Today, no living Australian can claim innocence, because Parliament has enacted the Native Title Amendment Act on behalf of the majority of this country, and that's the biggest single act of dispossession in our lifetime.

'I think there is a wide vein of guilt, but I see a real anger directed at us – a resentment that we didn't die out when we were supposed to. You've got to ask yourself: why haven't we been allowed to have just one victory? What's the matter? Is it because a proper acknowledgement of us, with full justice, would mean having to abandon the rubbish that we are inferior and having to accept that the foundation of white society is deeply flawed, and that there's another Australia?'[71]

Mick's brother, Pat, is quieter, but no less angry. Sent to a Roman Catholic missionary school, he was ordained in his twenties as the first Aboriginal Catholic priest. But his Aboriginality conflicted with the hierarchy of the Church; and put in charge of a mission near Darwin, he was criticised for introducing reforms that restored Aboriginal ceremonials. He left the priesthood and joined the land rights movement, and his fine bushy beard and broad-brimmed hat are familiar to many Australians, including politicians who foolishly have sought to exploit and co-opt him, mistaking his 'moderation' for generosity and a willingness to forgive that is part of Aboriginality.

When I first met Pat in Alice Springs, he described Aboriginal strength as 'built on the fact that we are unique survivors. You see, after years of holocaust . . . there is a certain genius not extinguished within us, despite what has happened to us. [It's] not a genius in the sense of being highly intellectual, but in the sense of something special in us that needs to be nurtured and cultivated and brought more and more into the light.' He was referring to the human spirit.[72]

Many white Australians care deeply about this Australian

injustice. There has been research showing that a clear majority want 'good relations' with the first nation.[73] Of course, this is not enough. Nor is it enough to plant a 'sea of hands' and sign 'sorry books' and join a great march of solidarity across Sydney Harbour Bridge. Nor is it enough to seek 'reconciliation', a problematic term when used against a background of violent occupation and theft. Only justice and a political will can end Australia's enduring disgrace.

The first step is a treaty, a native bill of rights that overrides the states and guarantees land rights and a proper share of resources. Opposition to this is the denialists' political motivation; it is what their government friends fear; for it will mean regarding Aborigines as both equals and special. At least twenty-seven other nation states have offered justice to their indigenous peoples in treaty and other forms. 'Both Canada and the United States,' wrote Colin Tatz, 'have accorded "first nation" status to Indians, recognising them as people who had prior occupation, sovereignty and governance, and have engaged them in true conversation about renegotiating treaties, compacts.'[74]

While neighbouring New Zealand has enacted land and sea rights for the Maori people, in Australia the Howard Government spends millions of dollars mounting technical arguments in the courts against the same land and sea rights. In 2001 there was one significant victory, however. The Northern Territory's mandatory Sentencing Act, which sent Aboriginal children to prison for stealing biscuits and which the UN had described as racist, was repealed shortly after the territory's redneck administration was voted out.

In 2002, flags bedecked Australia's tabloids as troops, led by the local SAS, joined the Americans for the 'war on terrorism' in

Afghanistan. No one knows what they are doing there; Australia is not at war with any country. But it is at war with refugees heading for its shores. Prior to September 11, 2001 the heroic SAS was assigned to prevent traumatised men, women and children from landing, then steered them to remote Pacific islands (where several contracted malaria). Many of those who have succeeded in reaching Australia receive treatment which, for a society proclaiming humanist values, beggars belief.

Imprisoned behind razor wire in some of the most hostile terrain on earth, in what, by any definition, are concentration camps, run by an American company specialising in top-security jails (profit: $387 million a year), the refugees, in their desperation, have resorted to suicide, starvation, arson and mass escapes. One study reveals that most had experienced terrible suffering before fleeing their homelands. Of thirty-three inmates questioned, nineteen had been tortured; nine had lost, through murder or 'disappearance', at least one immediate member of their family. 'On many occasions,' wrote Robert Manne, a professor at LaTrobe University in Melbourne, 'the refugees had been required to visit the horror of such experiences in interrogations by ignorant officials who make it transparent they do not believe the stories they are told.'[75] The refugees' life consists of daily musters and nightly headcounts, at 2am and 5am, under a regime of arbitrary punishments that range from the denial of visitors and telephone calls to solitary confinement, and worse.

Australians caught a glimpse of these horrors perpetrated in their name when an Australian Broadcasting Corporation programme told the story of a six-year-old Iranian boy, Shayan Badraie. Having spent a quarter of his life behind the wire of Woomera camp in the South Australian desert, he had seen desperate adults set themselves on fire and watched a suicidal man slash himself. 'I think he is dead,' he had told his father, who said these words were the last he uttered. Silent and depressed, he refused food and drink and sat day after day, drawing pictures of razor wire.

The minister responsible for the camps is Philip Ruddock, the same man who boasted to me that Aboriginal infant mortality was 'only' three times that of white children. Asked about Shayan Badraie on television, he referred to the boy as 'it' and 'the young man' and suggested that his problems stemmed from the fact that the woman in his family was not his real mother. The best thing for the boy was fostering, he said, implying that his father would be sent back to Iran.[76]

The falsehood of the political and popular fear around the issue of refugees is exposed by the fact that Australia receives one of the smallest number of 'illegal' asylum seekers in the world: about 4,000 a year. Of these, three-quarters are eventually accepted, but only after indefinite imprisonment in camps described by the former conservative prime minister, Malcolm Fraser, as 'hell-holes'. When an official of Amnesty International told Ruddock about the appalling conditions in the camps on the Pacific island of Nauru, whose government Australia has bribed to take its boat people, the minister's jocular reply was: 'Do you think they would prefer to be at one of *our* detention centres here?'[77]

The treatment of 'white' illegal immigrants is very different. In 2001, there were 6,160 Britons who had overstayed the duration of their visas, and as many other Europeans. More than 14,000 are caught by the authorities every year; none goes to a detention camp. They are given a 'bridging visa' that allows them time to earn enough for the fare home.

It is said that the 'tough stand' against the combined 'threat' posed by helpless refugees and unseen terrorists gave John Howard's Government its election victory in November 2001. 'Is Australia safe?' was the plaintive headline in the Melbourne *Age*.[78] There is a correlation between this false hysteria in what is perhaps the safest place on the planet and the 'tough stand' taken against the Aboriginal people, a minority of around 2 per cent of the population.

When an Aboriginal boxer, Anthony Mundine, remarked on television that Americans had 'brought [terrorism] upon themselves [for] what they done in the history of time', he was all but lynched. He is a Muslim. Thanks to his 'traitorous talk', crowed one of the media lynch party, 'Word is that his promising international career is over.'[79]

The tragedy for Australians seeking personal pride in the achievements of their nation is their ignorance of a politically distinctive past of which there is much to be proud, and whose wonderfully subversive stories that shaped the national character are seldom told. In the silver and zinc mines of Broken Hill, New South Wales, the miners won the world's first thirty-five-hour week, half a century ahead of Europe and America. Long before most of the world, Australia had a minimum wage, child benefits, pensions and the vote for women. By the 1960s, Australians could boast the most equitable spread of income in the world. The secret ballot was invented in Australia. And in my lifetime, Australia has been transformed from a second-hand Anglo-Irish society to one of the most culturally diverse places on earth, and it has happened peacefully. No matter that it may have happened by default in a country where the 'White Australia policy' ran so deep that one Australian prime minister, Billy Hughes, was the only leader who refused to sign an international declaration that recognised all races as being equal. Given this past, and by most standards of civilisation, the transformation is a remarkable achievement.

Of course, the first Australians were never included. Their extraordinary civilisation and their oneness with an ancient land were never taught as a source of national pride. And their inclusion, still to be achieved, remains the nation's key to itself.

Some years ago, I met the Aboriginal leader Rob Riley, an unforgettable man with a broad, wry smile, thick black beard and horn-rimmed glasses. Eloquent and witty, he spoke hard truths with a gentle voice. Despairing of having to 'climb into the gutter with the politicians', he later took his own life, like so many of his people. We had talked about the constant celebration of Australian 'nationhood' in historical anniversaries, the republican campaign and great sporting events. 'But it's simple,' he said. 'Unless you give us back our nationhood, you can never claim your own.'[80]

NOTES

INTRODUCTION

1 George Orwell, *Nineteen Eighty-Four*, London: Secker & Warburg, 1949.

2 United Nations Development Report figures, cited in *The Guardian*, October 22, 2001.

3 Interviewed by the author, Washington, January 2001.

4 Interviewed by the author, Jakarta, November 2000.

5 *New York Times*, June 19, 1966.

6 Boris Kagarlitsky, 'Facing the Crisis', *Links*, no. 19, September–December 2001.

7 *Independent on Sunday*, December 9, 2001.

8 Marc Herold, University of New Hampshire, cited by Seumas Milne in *The Guardian*, December 20, 2001.

9 *Socialist Worker*, January 19, 2002.

10 *Sydney Morning Herald*, December 29, 2001.

11 *The Guardian*, September 21, 2001.

12 *Independent*, November 1, 1998; David Holmes and Norm Dixon, *Behind the US War in Afghanistan*, Sydney: Resistance Books, 2001, pp. 47–52.

13 John K Cooley, *Unholy Wars: Afghanistan, America and International Terrorism*, London: Pluto Press, 2001.

14 *Observer*, December 9, 2001. David Astor's editorial appeared on November 4, 1956.

15 John Mueller and Karl Mueller, 'The Methodology of Mass Destruction: Assessing Threats in a New World Order', *The Journal of Strategic Studies*, vol. 23, no. 1, 2000, pp. 163–87.

16 United Nations Children's Fund (Unicef) and the Government of Iraq, *Child and Maternal Mortality Survey 1999: Preliminary Report*, 1999.

17 Interviewed by the author, New York, December 1999.

18 *The Guardian*, November 29, 2001.

19 *Green Left Weekly*, December 12, 2001.

20 United States Space Command, *Vision for 2020*, Director of Plans, Petersen AFB, Colorado; www.spacecom.af.mil/usspace

21 Cited in *Guardian Weekly*, January 3–9, 2002.

22 Ibid.

23 Samuel P Huntington, *The Clash of Civilisations*, New York: Simon & Schuster, 1996; Victor Davis Hanson, *Why the West Has Won: Carnage and Culture from Salamis to Vietnam*, London: Faber & Faber, 2001.

24 Marcela Lopez Levy, 'The damn water is ours!', *New Internationalist*, September 2001.

25 *Beyond the Barricades*, photographs selected by Omar Badsha, Gideon Mendel and Paul Weinberg, London: Kliptown Books, 1989, p. 71.

26 Gallup International, London, October 2001; www.gallup-international.com/surveys.htm

27 UN estimate of deaths from hunger, cited in *The Guardian*, October 22, 2001.

28 Robin Theurkauf, 'Are we at war?', *The Friend*, September 28, 2001.

THE MODEL PUPIL

1 World Bank reports, September 1997 and March 1998, cited in *Focus on the Global South*, CUSRI, Chulalongkorn University, Bangkok, Thailand: www.focusweb.org

2 Carlton Television, *The New Rulers of the World*, broadcast on ITV, July 18, 2001.

3 The Gap 'code of conduct' can be found online on the US Labor Department site: www.dol.org

4 World Bank, *Confidential Assessment Corrupted Bank Funds: Summary of RSI staff views regarding the problem of 'leakage' from World Bank project budgets*, Jakarta, August 1997.

5 Carmel Budiardjo and Liem Soei Liong, *The War against East Timor*, London: Zed Books, 1984, p. 49.

6 Gough Whitlam, *Abiding Interests*, St Lucia: University of Queensland Press, 1997, p. 71.

7 *Australian Financial Review*, May 17, 1994.

8 *Canberra Times*, May 15, 1996.

9 Joint Standing Committee on Foreign Affairs, Defence and Trade, *Australia's Relations with Indonesia*, Canberra: Australian Government Publishing Service, 1993, p. 96.

10 See John Pilger, 'Flying the Flag, Arming the World', *Hidden Agendas*, London: Vintage, 1998.

11 See John Pilger, 'East Timor', *Distant Voices*, London: Vintage, 1994.

12 International Monetary Fund, Letter of Intent (Indonesia), para. 86, January 20, 2000.

13 Brewster Keen, chief executive of Cargill, cited by John Madeley in *New Statesman*, May 22, 2000.

14 Central Intelligence Agency, Directorate of Intelligence, *Intelligence Report: Indonesia 1965, The Coup That Backfired*, Langley: CIA, 1968. See also *San Francisco Examiner*, May 20, 1990; *Washington Post*, May 21, 1990.

15 Gabriel Kolko, *Confronting the Third World*, New York: Pantheon, 1988, p. 181.

16 Peter Dale Scott, 'The United States and the Overthrow of Sukarno, 1965–1967', *Pacific Affairs*, no. 58, summer 1985.

17 Christopher J Koch, *The Year of Living Dangerously*, London: Minerva, 1978, p. 132.

18 HW Arndt, 'A comment', *Australian Outlook*, vol. 22, no. 1, April 1968, pp. 92–5.

19 Scott Burchill, *AQ: Journal of Contemporary Analysis*, vol. 73, issue 3, May–June 2001. See Greg Sheridan, *The Australian*, May 20, 1998; also *The Australian Review of Books*, December 2000.

20 *The Australian*, February 14, 1994.

21 Ibid., February 18 and 19, 1994.

22 Brian Toohey, *Sun-Herald*, Sydney, March 8, 1998. Toohey wrote, 'Kelly, who is now *The Australian*'s International Editor, was appointed to a new government body, the Foreign Affairs Council, which is chaired by Downer. The council's job is to advise the government on foreign policy, placing Kelly in the curious position of being an official government adviser at the same time as being a journalist commenting on government policy.'

23 *The Australian*, February 25, 1998.

24 Mark Curtis, *The Ambiguities of Power: British Foreign Policy since 1945*, London: Zed Books, 1995, p. 57.

25 *The Times*, August 8, 1986; cited by Paul Lashmar and James Oliver in *Britain's Secret Propaganda War 1948–1977*, London: Sutton, 1998, p. 4.

26 Harold Crouch, *The Army and Politics in Indonesia*, Ithaca: Cornell University Press, 1997, pp. 155 and 351.

27 *San Francisco Examiner*, May 20, 1990; *Washington Post*, May 21, 1990.

28 Ibid.

29 Ibid.

30 Photograph secured by Tapol, the Indonesia Human Rights Organisation, London.

31 US National Archives, RG 59 Records of Department of State: cable no. 868, ref: Embtel 852, October 5, 1965.

32 *San Francisco Examiner*, May 20, 1990.

33 Letter from Andrew Gilchrist to EH Peck, head of the South-East Asia Division at the Foreign Office, October 5, 1965.

34 Cable from the British embassy in Jakarta to POLAD (Political Adviser) Singapore, no. 1835, October 6, 1965.

35 Letter from GFN Reddaway to Andrew Gilchrist, Singapore, July 18, 1966.

36 Roland Challis, *Shadow of a Revolution*, London: Sutton, 2001, p. 102.

37 Interview with the author, *The New Rulers of the World* (see n. 2).

38 *Time*, July 15, 1966; *US News and World Report*, June 6, 1966; *New York Times*, June 19, 1966.

39 *New York Times*, July 6, 1966.

40 David Goldsworthy, David Dutton, Peter Gifford and Roderic Petty, *Facing North: A Century of Australian Engagement with Asia, Volume 1: 1901 to the 1970s*, Department of Foreign Affairs and Trade, Melbourne: Melbourne University Press, 2001, pp. 354, 355.

41 Ibid., p. 354.

42 Ibid., pp. 354–5.

43 Letter from Andrew Gilchrist to the Foreign Office, February 23, 1977; cited in *Tapol Bulletin,* no. 163, October 2001.

44 *Tapol Bulletin,* no. 159, August/September 2000.

45 Interview with the author, Jakarta, December 12, 2000.

46 Dale Scott, 'The United States and the Overthrow of Sukarno' (see n. 16).

47 Interview with the author, 1982.

48 David Ransom, 'The Berkeley Mafia and the Indonesian Massacre', *Ramparts,* no. 4, October 1970.

49 Interview with the author, Jakarta, December 10, 2000.

50 *To Aid in the Rebuilding of a Nation*, Proceedings of the Indonesian Investment Conference report, Geneva, November 2–4, 1967 (LBJ Library. With thanks to Bradley R Simpson).

51 Letter from James A Linen to General Suharto, March 22, 1967 (LBJ Library).

52 James A Linen, 'An International Meeting to Establish a Creative Dialogue for Future Commitments', Proceedings of the Indonesian Investment Conference report, Geneva (see n. 50).

53 Interview with the author, *The New Rulers of the World* (see n. 2).

54 Letters from President Lyndon Johnson to James A Linen, December 1 and 23, 1967 (LBJ Library).

55 Kei C Yamato, 'The Pacific-Asia World: Profit Opportunities and Challenges for US Business', *Gallatin Special Report*, December 1967.

56 *The New Rulers of the World* (see n. 2).

57 Ransom, 'The Berkeley Mafia' (see n. 48).

58 Study by Morgan Dean Witter, *Sydney Morning Herald*, February 24, 2001.

PAYING THE PRICE

1 Interview with the author, Basra, October 18, 1999.

2 Ibid.

3 Interview with the author, January 14, 2000.

4 Carlton Television, *Paying the Price: Killing the Children of Iraq*, broadcast on ITV, March 6, 2000.

5 *British Medical Journal*, January 16, 1999.

6 *Paying the Price* (see n. 4).

7 Ibid.

8 Ibid.

9 Ibid.

10 Ibid.

11 Ibid.

12 *Washington Post*, June 23, 1999.

13 *New York Times*, June 3, 1991.

14 Asherio and others, 'Special Article: Effects of the Gulf War on Infant and Child Mortality in Iraq', *New England Journal of Medicine*, September 24, 1992.

15 *New York Times*, June 2, 1991.

16 Eric Herring, 'Between Iraq and a hard place: a critique of the British government's case for UN economic sanctions', *Review of International Studies 2002*, pp. 40–41.

17 See the UN website: www.un.org/Docs/scres/1999/99scrs687.htm

18 United Nations, *Report of the Executive Chairman on the Activities of the Special Commission Established by the Secretary-General Pursuant to Paragraph 9 (b) of Resolution 687, 1991*, October 6, 1998.

19 Letter from the UN Secretary-General to the President of the Security Council, December 15, 1998.

20 *Paying the Price* (see n. 4).

21 Agence France Presse, November 3, 1999.

22 See Paul Conlon, *United Nations Sanctions Management: a Case Study of the Iraq Sanctions Committee, 1990–1994*, New York: Transnational Publishers, 2000, pp. 73–4.

23 United Nations Office of the Iraq Programme (Oil for Food), *Weekly Update*, New York, October 16, 2001.

24 Speech by French Foreign Minister Hubert Vedrine, *Morning Star*, August 3, 2000.

25 Standard Foreign Office letter signed by Jamie Cooper, Middle East Department, March 27, 2000.

26 United Nations, *Report of the Secretary-General Pursuant to Paragraph 5 of Security Council Resolution 1281 (1999)*, June 1, 2000.

27 United Nations, *Briefing by Benon Sevan, Executive Director of the Iraq Programme, at the Informal Consultations Held by the Security Council*, July 22, 1999.

28 *Washington Post*, January 28, 1999.

29 Letter from John Ashworth, Chairman of the British Library, to Harry Cohen MP, June 30, 1999.

30 *The Guardian*, February 18, 2000.

31 Interview with the author, Baghdad, October 17, 1999.

32 *Green Left Weekly* (Sydney), June 21, 2000.

33 In conversation with the author, January 16, 2001.

34 United Nations Children's Fund (Unicef) and the Government of Iraq, *Child and Maternal Mortality Survey 1999: Preliminary Report*, 1999.

35 *Toronto Star*, June 25, 2000.

36 In conversation with the author, May 4, 2000.

37 *The Guardian*, April 1, 1999.

38 'The Public Health Impact of Sanctions', *Middle East Report*, no. 215, summer 2000, p. 17. (Garfield is Professor of Clinical International Nursing at Columbia University, New York.)

39 John Mueller and Karl Mueller, 'The Methodology of Mass Destruction: Assessing Threats in a New World Order', *The Journal of Strategic Studies*, vol. 23, no. 1, 2000, pp. 163–87.

40 *Philadelphia Inquirer*, February 14, 2000.

41 'Punishing Saddam', *60 Minutes*, CBS Television, May 12, 1996.

42 See John Pilger, 'Mythmakers of the Gulf War', *Distant Voices*, London: Vintage, 1994.

43 State Department document, 1945, cited by Joyce and Gabriel Kolko in *The Limits of Power*, New York: Harper & Row, 1972, p. 242.

44 Andrew Cockburn and Patrick Cockburn, *Out of the Ashes: the Resurrection of Saddam Hussein*, New York: HarperCollins, 1999, p. 74.

45 *Paying the Price* (see n. 4).

46 Cockburn and Cockburn, *Out of the Ashes*, p. 83 (see n. 44).

47 Roger Normand, 'Sanctions against Iraq: New Weapon of Mass Destruction', *Covert Action Quarterly*, Washington, spring 1998.

48 Cockburn and Cockburn, *Out of the Ashes*, pp. 89–90 (see n. 44).

49 *The Guardian,* May 2 and 8, 1992. See also US General Accounting Office, *IRAQ: US Military Items Exported or Transferred to Iraq in the 1980s,* February 1994.

50 US Senate, Committee on Banking, Housing and Urban Affairs, *US Chemical and Biological Warfare-Related Dual Use Exports to Iraq and Their Possible Impact on the Health Consequences of the Persian Gulf War*, May 25, 1994. See also US Department of Commerce,

Bureau of Finance Administration, *Approved Licences to Iraq*, March 11, 1991.

51 *Paying the Price* (see n. 4).

52 *The Guardian*, May 8, 1992.

53 Interview with the author, for Central Television, *Flying the Flag, Arming the World,* broadcast on ITV, 1994.

54 Interview with the author, October 1999.

55 *Hansard,* December 21, 1999.

56 Interview with the author, October 2001.

57 Ibid.

58 *Paying the Price* (see n. 4).

59 Ibid.

60 Figures supplied to Christopher Martin, associate producer of *Paying the Price* (see n. 4), by Captain Amy Bailey, Department of Defence, Washington, February 19, 2000. The period covered is from May 31, 1998 to January 14, 2000. As a comparative figure, 18,276 sorties were flown by US aircraft during the Gulf War: same source.

61 *Boston Globe*, December 11, 1999; CNN, December 28, 1999.

62 *The Guardian*, November 11, 2000.

63 *New York Times*, August 13, 1999.

64 *Washington Post*, March 12, 1998.

65 Independent Television News, April 4, 1991.

66 In correspondence and conversation with the author, March 3–4, 2001.

67 *Washington Post*, October 25, 2000.

68 Cockburn and Cockburn, *Out of the Ashes*, p. 13 (see n. 44).

69 *Paying the Price* (see n. 4).

70 Cockburn and Cockburn, *Out of the Ashes*, p. 23 (see n. 44).

71 Ibid., pp. 24–5.

72 Ibid., p. 29.

73 *Green Left Weekly*, October 24, 2001.

74 Ibid.

75 Interview on *ABC News*, cited by Sarah Graham-Brown in *Sanctioning Saddam*, London/New York: IB Tauris, 1999, p. 19.

76 Cited by Herring, 'Between Iraq and a hard place' (see n. 16).

77 *New York Times*, July 7, 1991.

78 *New Statesman*, March 19, 2001.

79 *Wall Street Journal*, October 22, 1999.

80 Peter Gowan, 'Neoliberal Cosmopolitanism', *New Left Review*, September/October 2001.

81 Interview with the author, Washington, November 29, 1999.

82 Interview with the author, New York, December 2, 1999.

83 Interview with the author, New York, December 2, 1999.

84 The multiple claims and counter-claims by government ministers and opponents of sanctions are digested in *Voices*, the excellent newsletter of Voices in the Wilderness, available from 16B Cherwell Road, Oxford, OX4 1BG. See also *New Statesman*, March 27, 2000 and articles from *New Statesman* thereafter, posted on www.johnpilger.com; also *The Guardian*, January 8, 2001. The UN document quoted by Hans Von Sponeck, refuting Peter Hain's claim of $16 billion worth of relief, is S/2000/1132, November 29, 2000. George Somerwill was quoted in the *Toronto Star*, June 24, 2000.

85 The *Independent*, June 5, 1999, citing a confidential memorandum from the UK Atomic Energy Authority to Royal Ordnance, April 30, 1991.

86 Cited in Campaign against Sanctions on Iraq (CASI), *Starving Iraq: One Humanitarian Disaster We Can Stop*, Cambridge, pp. 5–6.

87 *Iraq: Country Report 1995–96, Economist* Intelligence Unit, London, p. 6.

88 Roger Normand, 'Sanctions against Iraq: New Weapon of Mass Destruction', *Covert Action Quarterly*, spring 1998.

89 Arthur Miller, 'Why I Wrote *The Crucible*: An Artist's Answer to Politics', *New Yorker*, October 21–28, 1996, pp. 163–4.

90 *Paying the Price* (see n. 4).

91 Interview with the author, December 3, 1999.

92 *New Statesman*, January 15, 2001.

93 Marc Bossuyt, *The Adverse Consequences of Economic Sanctions on the Enjoyment of Human Rights*, Working Paper, UN Economic and Social Council Sub-Commission on the Promotion and Protection of Human Rights, June 21, 2000.

94 *New Statesman*, January 22, 2001, following correspondence with the author.

95 Interview with the author, Baghdad, October 24, 1999.

THE GREAT GAME

1 *Independent on Sunday*, February 10, 1991.

2 Press Association, November 2, 2001.

3 BBC *News*, November 19, 2001.

4 *Independent*, November 19, 2001.

5 *The Guardian*, November 29, 2001.

6 *Independent*, September 19, 2001; *Financial Times*, September 20, 2001; *Daily Telegraph*, October 3 and 4, 2001; *The Times*, October 8, 2001.

7 Human Rights Watch, New York, October 6, 2001.

8 *Sydney Morning Herald*, February 11, 2002.

9 *The Guardian*, November 15, 2001.

10 BBC World Service, September 22, 2001.

11 Cited in the *Rock River Times*, Rockford, Illinois, October 31–November 6, 2001.

12 John Rees, 'Imperialism: Globalisation, the State and War', *International Socialism*, issue 93, p. 13.

13 *US News and World Report*, September 29, 1997.

14 *International Herald Tribune*, November 9, 1998.

15 *Daily Telegraph*, October 11, 1996.

16 Cited by Lance Selfa, *International Socialist Review*, issue 20, November–December 2001.

17 *The Guardian*, October 23, 2001.

18 Ibid.

19 Cited in the *Rock River Times*, October 24–30, 2001.

20 *Wall Street Journal* and Judicial Watch: www.azlan.net/jud-watch.htm

21 *The Guardian*, November 5, 2001.

22 Frank Furedi, *The New Ideology of Imperialism*, London: Pluto Press, 1994, p. 44.

23 Zbigniew Brzezinski, *The Grand Chessboard: American Primacy and its Geostrategic Imperatives*, New York: HarperCollins, 1997, p. xiii.

24 Ibid., p. 53.

25 Ibid., p. 73.

26 Ibid., p. 40.

27 *New York Times*, October 19, 2001.

28 Cited in *New Statesman*, December 22, 2000–January 3, 2001.

29 *New Statesman*, October 22, 2001.

30 Boris Kagarlitsky, 'Facing the Crisis', *Links*, no. 19, September–December 2001.

31 *New Statesman*, November 26, 2001.

32 Rees, 'Imperialism: Globalisation, the State and War', pp. 23–4 (see n. 12).

33 World Bank, *World Development Indicators*, April 2001; see www.developmentgoals.org

34 Jeremy Rifkin, *The End of Work: The Decline of the Global Labor Force and the Dawn of the Post-Market Era*, New York: Tarcher/Putnam, 1995, pp. 205–7.

35 Cited by Walden Bello, with Shea Cunningham and Bill Rau, in *Dark Victory: the United States, Structural Adjustment and Global Poverty*, London: Pluto Press, 1994, p. 51; United Nations Development Programme, *Human Development Report 1996*, Oxford: Oxford University Press, p. 19.

36 Michael McKinley, *Triage: a Survey of the 'New Inequality' as Combat Zone*, presentation to 42nd Annual Convention of the International Studies Association, Chicago, February 2001.

37 *New York Times*, September 3, 1995.

38 *Green Left Weekly*, October 17, 2001.

39 In conversation with the author, November 2001.

40 George Monbiot, *The Guardian*, November 6, 2001.

41 Christian Aid at www.christian-aid.org.uk. See Department of International Development press releases, December 11, 2000; March 19, 2001; November 7, 2001.

42 Christian Aid, *Trading in White Gold: who decides Ghana's water policy?*, London, October 2001.

43 United States Space Command, *Vision for 2020*, Director of Plans, Petersen AFB, Colorado; www.spacecom.af.mil/usspace. With thanks to Karl Grossman for his investigative journalism.

44 As told to the author.

45 *Time*, December 28, 1992.

46 'CIA officials privately concede that the US military may have killed between 7,000 and 10,000 Somalis', cited by Noam Chomsky, *Z* magazine, summer 1995.

47 *The Guardian*, November 15, 2001.

48 *BBC Short Wave Broadcasts Summary*, June 2000.

49 *The Guardian*, October 26, 2001.

50 BBC Gulf War coverage, January 18, 1991.

51 *International Herald Tribune*, February 23–24, 1991; *New York Times*, January 15, 1992.

52 *Newsday*, September 12, 1991.

53 BBC, *The Late Show*, June 6, 1991.

54 Ramsey Clark, *The Fire This Time: US War Crimes in the Gulf*, New York: Thunder's Mouth Press, 1992, p. 42.

55 *New York Times*, January 26, 1992.

56 *Wall Street Journal*, March 22, 1991.

57 Ian Lee, *Continuing Health Cost of the Gulf War*, London: Medical Educational Trust, 1991.

58 *The Times* and *Le Nouvel Observateur*, March 3, 1991.

59 Clark, *The Fire This Time*, p. 110 (see n. 54).

60 *Observer*, October 28, 2001.

61 John Pilger, *Hidden Agendas*, London: Vintage, 1998, pp. 115–52.

62 *Breakfast with Frost*, BBC Television, September 30, 2001.

63 *The Guardian*, October 27, 2001. Author's contacts with company headquarters, Bethesda, Maryland, November 2001.

64 *Guardian Weekly,* December 20–26, 2001.

65 BBC Radio 4, November 6, 2001.

66 Richard Falk, 'The Terrorist Foundations of Recent US Policy', in *Western State Terrorism*, London: Macmillan, 1988, cited by Noam Chomsky in Alexander George, ed., *Western State Terrorism*, Cambridge: Polity Press, 1991, p. 12.

67 *New York Times*, September 22, 1998; Associated Press, September 20, 2001.

68 Associated Press, July 16, 1997, cited by William Blum in *Rogue State*, London: Zed Books, 2001, p. 80.

69 Ibid.

70 Ibid., pp. 80–81.

71 Ibid., p. 81.

72 George Monbiot in *The Guardian*, October 30, 2001.

73 Ibid.

74 Robert Cooper, cited by Tariq Ali in 'Our Herods', *New Left Review*, September/October 2000.

75 *The Guardian*, October 2, 2001. Thanks to Noam Chomsky for these quotes. See his latest work, *9–11*, New York: Seven Stories Press, 2001.

76 *Boston Globe*, August 22, 1999.

77 Werner Daum, 'Universalism and the West', *Harvard International Review*, summer 2001.

78 Christopher Hitchens, *Spectator*, September 29, 2001.

79 Health Information and Policy Institute, www.hdip.org/reports; The Union of Palestine Relief Committees, June 2001.

80 *Observer*, October 15, 2000.

81 *Hansard*, November 14, 2001.

82 Amnesty International, *News Review*, November/December 2000. See also Neil Sammonds, *British culpability and the shadow of Canary Wharf*, 2001, www.palestinecampaign.org; *Hansard*, November 17, 2000 and November 8, 2001.

83 *Jane's Foreign Report*, May and July 2001. See also Akiva Eldar, 'Big Pines II – Rumors are rife of an invasion plan', *Ha'aretz*, Tel Aviv, July 10, 2001.

84 Cited by Alexander Cockburn, 'The war they wanted', Creators Syndicate, Znet, www.zmag.org

85 *Yugoslavia: the Avoidable War*, a documentary film by George Bogdanich and Martin Lettmayer: see www.avoidablewar.com

86 Ibid.

87 *New Statesman*, September 4, 2000, and others; John Pilger, *Distant Voices*, London: Vintage, 1994, pp. 213–19; Michel Chossudovsky, *The Globalisation of Poverty: Impacts of IMF and World Bank Reforms*, London: Pluto Press, pp. 243–64.

88 Cited in *New Statesman*, November 12, 2001.

89 Channel 4 *News*, November 2, 2001; *New York Times*, December 4, 2001.

90 *Observer*, November 11, 2001.

91 *The Guardian*, October 10, 2001.

92 *The Guardian*, September 19, 2001; *Independent, The Times* and *Financial Times*, September 20, 2001.

93 *New York Times*, May 6, 1978.

94 *Wall Street Journal*, January 6, 1979.

95 *Washington Post*, June 1, 1979.

96 *Observer*, September 30, 2001.

97 Cited by David Holmes and Norm Dixon in *Behind the US War in Afghanistan*, Sydney: Resistance Books, 2001, p. 27.

98 *Le Nouvel Observateur*, January 15–21, 1998.

99 Holmes and Dixon, *Behind the US War*, p. 29 (see n. 97).

100 *Independent*, November 1, 1998; Ahmed Rashid, of the *Far Eastern Economic Review*, cited by Holmes and Dixon, *Behind the US War*, p. 49. (Thanks to Holmes and Dixon for much of this research.)

101 *The Guardian*, October 31, 2001.

102 Chomsky, *9–11*, p. 15 (see n. 75).

103 *Observer*, January 10, 1993.

104 *The Guardian*, October 24, 2001.

105 Timothy Dunne, 'Liberalism', in John Baylis and Steve Smith, eds, *The Globalisation of World Politics: an Introduction to International Relations*, Oxford: Oxford University Press, 1997, pp. 147–63.

106 David Edwards, 'Arms, Climate Change and the Grand Media Deception', medialens@yahoogroups.com, February 2002.

THE CHOSEN ONES

1 *Sydney Morning Herald*, September 30, 1993; *Guardian Weekly*, October 3, 1993; *The Weekend Australian*, January 30–31, 1999.

2 Related to the author by the late Charles Perkins, then a member of an Olympic Games advisory panel.

3 *PM*, ABC Radio, July 16, 1993.

4 B Thylefors et al, 'WHO Data on Blindness', in *Ophthalmic Epidemiology*, The Netherlands: Aeolus Press, 1995, vol. 2, no. 1, pp. 5–39.

5 *Sydney Morning Herald*, January 31, 1998.

6 Interview with the author, Perth, December 1998.

7 Interview with the author, Kununurra, December 1998; Richard Murray, *Aboriginal Primary Health Care – an Evidence Based Approach,* Oxford: Oxford University Press, 1999.

8 Interview with the author, Queensland, December 1998.

9 Interview with the author, Queensland, December 1998.

10 Report by the Australian Bureau of Statistics, cited in *Sydney Morning Herald*, April 3, 1997.

11 Dr Ben Bartlett, *Djadi Dugarang*, newsletter of the Indigenous Social Justice Association, reprinted in *Green Left Weekly*, November 4, 1998.

12 Aboriginal and Torres Strait Islander Social Justice Commissioner, *Second Report*, Canberra, 1994, p. 99.

13 Murray, *Aboriginal Primary Health Care* (see n. 7).

14 *Canberra Times*, May 28, 1997.

15 Interview with the author, December 1998.

16 *Sydney Morning Herald*, March 16, 1999.

17 *Sydney Morning Herald*, September 23, 1996.

18 Ibid., April 22, 1997.

19 Ibid., May 31, 1997.

20 Jan Roberts, *Massacres to Mining: the Colonisation of Aboriginal Australia*, Melbourne: Dove Communications, 1981, p. 47.

21 *Sydney Morning Herald*, April 30, 1997.

22 *National Times*, March 29–April 4, 1985.

23 Ibid.

24 *The Age*, December 28, 1996.

25 *Canberra Times*, January 5, 1997.

26 Martin Taylor, *Bludgers in Grass Castles: Native Title and the Unpaid Debts of the Pastoral Industry*, Sydney: Resistance Books, 1997.

27 Ibid.

28 Sir Ralph Cilento and Clem Lack, *Triumph in the Tropics*, p. 179, cited in Ross Fitzgerald, *A History of Queensland from 1915 to the 1980s*, University of Queensland Press, 1984, p. 552.

29 Interview with the author, Roma, Queensland, December 1998.

30 *The Australian*, June 9, 1997.

31 Anti-Slavery Society, *Land and Justice: Aborigines Today*, London, June 1987, p. 2.

32 Letter from Henry Reynolds to the author, June 18, 1998. See also Henry Reynolds, 'The Mabo Judgement in the Light of Imperial Land Policy', *UNNSW Law Journal*, vol. 16, issue 1, 1993.

33 *Sydney Morning Herald*, March 16, 1999.

34 *Mail and Guardian*, Johannesburg, March 19–20, 1999.

35 Human Rights and Equal Opportunity Commission, *Bringing Them Home: National Inquiry into the Separation of Aboriginal and Torres Strait Islander Children from Their Families*, Sydney, April 1997.

36 On February 22, 1933, the Secretary of the Department of the Interior in Canberra, JA Carrodus, wrote, 'The policy of mating half-castes with whites for the purpose of breeding out the colour is that adopted by the Commonwealth Government on the recommendation of Dr Cook [the architect of Aboriginal policy in the Northern Territory].' Cited by Robert Manne, *Sydney Morning Herald*, March 22, 1999.

37 The work of historians Rosalind Kidd, Heather Goodall and Peter Read, cited in *Sydney Morning Herald*, June 30, 1971.

38 Russel Ward, *Man Makes History: World History from the Earliest Times to the Renaissance — for Boys and Girls in the First Year of Secondary School Courses*, Sydney: Shakespeare Head Press, 1952, p. 9.

39 *The Australian School Atlas*, Melbourne: Oxford University Press, 1939, pp. vii, 51–62.

40 Cited in Roberts, *Massacres to Minining,* p. 68 (see n. 20).

41 Interview with the author, Sydney, December 1998.

42 Interview with the author, Sydney, November 1998.

43 Colin Tatz, *Obstacle Race: Aborigines in Sport*, Sydney: University of New South Wales Press, 1995, p. 62.

44 Donald Bradman, *Farewell to Cricket*, London: Theodore Brun, 1950, pp. 48, 288, cited in Tatz, *Obstacle Race*, p. 77.

45 Thom Blake, *A Dumping Ground: Barambah Aboriginal Settlement 1900–40*, PhD thesis, University of Queensland, 1991, p. 340, cited in Tatz, *Obstacle Race,* p. 77.

46 Blake, *A Dumping Ground*, cited in Tatz, *Obstacle Race*, p. 79.

47 Tatz, *Obstacle Race,* pp. 95–6 (see n. 43).

48 Ibid., p. 126.

49 Interview with the author, Sydney, December 1998.

50 Interview with the author, Sydney, November 1998.

51 Colin Tatz, *Genocide in Australia*, Australian Institute of

Aboriginal and Torres Strait Islander Studies, December 1998.

52 *West Australian*, June 17, 1997.

53 *Sydney Morning Herald*, February 25, 1987.

54 *The Age*, November 27, 1998.

55 Colin Tatz, '"It Didn't Happen": Depictions of Denial', in *Other than Human: the Armenian, Jewish and Aboriginal Experiences*, Sydney: Brandl & Schlesinger, forthcoming.

56 Ibid.

57 Ibid. See also *Sydney Morning Herald*, September 9, 14 and 19, 2000.

58 *Bulletin*, June 2001.

59 Tatz, 'It Didn't Happen' (see n. 55).

60 Interview with the author, November 1998.

61 *Sydney Morning Herald*, April 8, 1997.

62 Aboriginal and Torres Strait Islander Commission, *Indigenous Deaths in Custody 1989–1996*, Canberra, November 1996. Since then, the situation has not changed.

63 Interview with the author, November 1998.

64 *Sydney Morning Herald*, May 8, 1991.

65 Ibid., March 10, 1988.

66 Interview with the author, Sydney, June 1987.

67 Interview with the author, Sydney, November 1998.

68 Ibid.

69 *Sydney Morning Herald*, August 30, 2000.

70 Ibid., August 7, 2000.

71 Interview with the author, Sydney, November 1998.

72 Interview with the author, Sydney, June 1987.

73 *Sydney Morning Herald*, May 31, 1997.

74 Tatz, *Genocide in Australia* (see n. 51).

75 *Sydney Morning Herald*, December 10, 2001.

76 Cited by Bob Ellis in 'Frankly I do give a damn', *HQ*, October/November 2001.

77 *Sydney Morning Herald*, December 10, 2001.

78 *The Age*, October 17, 2001.

79 Miranda Devine, 'The Man cops a sucker punch from critics', *Sydney Morning Herald*, October 25, 2001.

80 Interview with the author, June 1987.

INDEX